ROBLOX

Written by Alex Cox and Alex Wiltshire
Edited by Craig Jelley
Designed by John Stuckey
Illustrations by John Stuckey, James Wood, and Ryan Marsh
Production by Louis Harvey
Special thanks to the entire Roblox team

All stats featured in this book were based on information publicly available on the Roblox
platform and were correct as of October 2018.

ISBN 978-0-06-288423-7
❖
19 20 21 22 23 RTLO 10 9 8 7 6 5 4 3 2
First US Edition, 2019

Original English language edition first published in 2019 by Egmont UK Limited,
The Yellow Building, 1 Nicholas Road, London, W11 4AN, United Kingdom.

Stay safe online. Any website addresses listed in this book are correct at the time of going
to print. However, HarperCollins is not responsible for content hosted by third parties.
Please be aware that online content can be subject to change and websites can contain
content that is unsuitable for children.We advise that all children are supervised
when using the internet.

TOP ROLE-PLAYING GAMES

HARPER

An Imprint of HarperCollins*Publishers*

CONTENTS

HELLO! 6-7

MEEPCITY 8-9

DINOSAUR SIMULATOR 10-11

WORK AT A PIZZA PLACE 12-13

ROBLOXIAN HIGHSCHOOL 14-15

ADOPT ME! 16-17

BOOGA BOOGA 18-19

FASHION FAMOUS 20-21

VEHICLE SIMULATOR 22-23

HOTEL ELEPHANT 24-25

PRISON LIFE 26-27

NIGHT OF THE WEREWOLF 28-29

THE NORTHERN FRONTIER 30-31

SUPER HERO LIFE II 32-33

HORSE WORLD 34-35

SORO'S ISLAND 36-37

THE PLAZA 38-39

WELCOME TO BLOXBURG 40-41

PICK A SIDE 42-43

MINING SIMULATOR 44-45

BAKERS VALLEY 46-47

ROYALE HIGH 48-49

ACTION! 50-51

ROBLOXIAN WATERPARK 52-53

PIRATE SIMULATOR 54-55

STYLZ MAKEOVER 56-57

WOLVES' LIFE 3 58-59

PIZZA FACTORY TYCOON 60-61

ROBLOX HIGH SCHOOL 62-63

VENTURELAND 64-65

FAIRY WORLD 66-67

TREASURE HUNT SIMULATOR 68-69

ROCITIZENS 70-71

SNOW SHOVELING SIMULATOR 72-73

TOP ROBLOX RUNWAY MODEL 74-75

BOOK OF MONSTERS 76-77

NATURAL DISASTER SURVIVAL 78-79

TRADE HANGOUT 80-81

VET SIMULATOR 82-83

RESTAURANT TYCOON 84-85

BUILD A BOAT FOR TREASURE 86-87

THE NEIGHBORHOOD OF ROBLOXIA 88-89

ACHIEVEMENT CHECKLIST 90-93

GOODBYE! 94-95

| HELLO!

WELL, HELLO THERE

Absolutely fabulous to meet you, my fellow Robloxian friend. Mr. Bling Bling is the name and partaking in incredible Roblox experiences is my game. If I'm correctly informed, you're interested in testing new Robloxian waters and trying your hand at as many different roles as you can. Excellent!

If that is indeed the case, you've come to the right place. Nobody has sampled more of the enticing games that Roblox has to offer than I. In this expertly curated volume, we have games that allow you to open a gourmet restaurant, others that will grant you magical powers and task you with saving cities, and others that will have you assume the role of beasts of all shapes and sizes. Whichever game you choose, they will surely have one thing in common – an immense amount of fun.

With my final words, I will share my advice for making the most of this selection of role-playing games. Make sure to be flexible, fearless, and, above all, friendly. You'll be interacting with others, so play nice and you'll have an excellent time and make some new friends.

MR. BLING BLING

MEEPCITY

Come and see the sights in the ever popular MeepCity! Have fun in the Playground, then visit the Plaza for a bite to eat before dancing the night away at a cool party. MeepCity is the perfect place for you and your new Meep pet to hang out and enjoy the city lifestyle!

In MeepCity, you get a place to call home in the Neighborhood. It may look small on the outside, but your estate offers you a fully customizable space to try out your interior design skills and create the perfect pad! 》》》

Beyond the Neighborhood, you'll find a Playground full of activities, a Plaza with a pizza place and ice-cream parlor, and a bustling city. There are shops to buy gear and plenty of locations, like the hospital, to role-play with friends and live life to the max. 》》

You can also challenge friends in a minigame. Speed around cool tracks in MeepCity Racing and earn coins as you leave your friends in your wake! Or you can try to set the best time on the Star Ball courses.

《《

GAME STATS

DEVELOPER: Alexnewtron
SUBGENRES: Town and City, Minigames
VISITS:
FAVORITED:

QUICK TIPS

COIN COLLECTOR

You earn coins, MeepCity's currency, as you spend time in the game. You can boost your bank balance by fishing at the pond and selling your catch of the day at the Pet Shop. You can also earn coins playing amazing minigames.

CITY SHORTCUT

Don't worry if you lose your bearings. Click on your profile screen in the top menu, and you'll be able to teleport to your favorite places, whether it's to jump into a game of Star Ball, or you just want to find your way home!

MEGA MORPH

You can experience MeepCity from another perspective with the morphing stations in the Playground. You can switch your character between child, teen, and adult forms so you can role-play all kinds of different scenarios.

PARTY TIME!

If you want to boogie, then go to the party tent in the Playground. You can join different types of parties, from gaming to fashion, or, if you have a MeepCity Plus pass, you can host your own get-together for your friends.

ALEXNEWTRON

Having dabbled on Roblox for more than a decade, developer Alexnewtron hit the heady heights of Roblox fame when MeepCity became the first experience to hit a billion visits. Below we hear about Alexnewtron's hints for starting out, his assets, and a top tip to make you the master of MeepCity.

ON GAMEPLAY

"It's easy to imagine what you want your game to look and feel like. So, when you start out you spend a lot of time polishing an aesthetic for your game," says Alexnewtron. "But that's before you know if anyone wants to play your game! It's important to create a functional game first, even if it's ugly. Then you can learn how players play your game... and then you can polish."

ON ORGANIZED OBJECTS

The way to a successful game is a tidy game, as Alexnewtron explains: "I always try to keep my objects in Roblox Studio as organized as possible, with lots of different folders that keep my assets ready to replicate to players as they join my game."

ON MEEPCITY SECRETS

How do you become a MeepCity legend? Alexnewtron reveals all: "Upgrade your fishing rod as soon as possible to increase your chances of catching rare fish and earning more coins! Also, be a friendly citizen. You can gift furniture to your pals even if they're offline. They'll receive the gift in their mailbox the next time they play."

DINOSAUR SIMULATOR

It's the age of the dinosaur and herds of giant reptiles roam the landscape searching for food and water. It's a dino-eat–dino world out there, and it takes a special kind of gamer to endure the rigors of prehistoric life. Are you ready to see if you have what it takes to survive extinction?

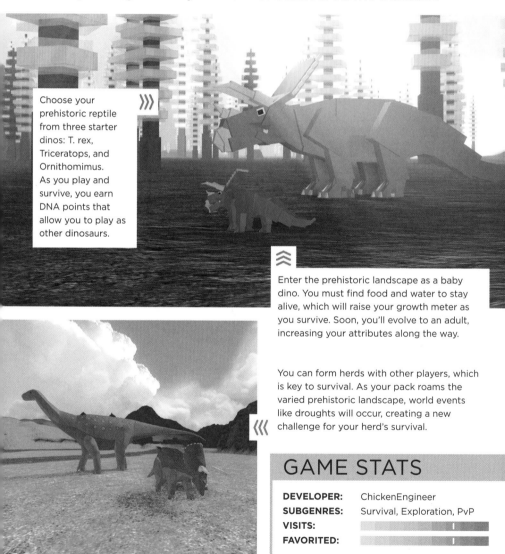

Choose your prehistoric reptile from three starter dinos: T. rex, Triceratops, and Ornithomimus. As you play and survive, you earn DNA points that allow you to play as other dinosaurs.

Enter the prehistoric landscape as a baby dino. You must find food and water to stay alive, which will raise your growth meter as you survive. Soon, you'll evolve to an adult, increasing your attributes along the way.

You can form herds with other players, which is key to survival. As your pack roams the varied prehistoric landscape, world events like droughts will occur, creating a new challenge for your herd's survival.

GAME STATS

DEVELOPER:	ChickenEngineer
SUBGENRES:	Survival, Exploration, PvP
VISITS:	
FAVORITED:	

QUICK TIPS

OMNIVORE
Pick your dinosaur carefully. Food can be hard to find, especially if you're carnivorous but not big enough to take down your own prey. However, if you are fast enough, you can scavenge the leftovers from other dinos!

EVOLUTION
You earn DNA points while you play the game and grow into an adult. You can spend your DNA from the main menu to unlock new dinosaur models to play with, including flying creatures and marine reptiles like the Liopleurodon.

DINO NAP
Having a rest is a good way to gain some percentage points (which you need in order to grow) without using too much energy. Make sure you don't neglect your food and drink meters while you're fast asleep though!

FAMILY STONE-AGE
When you finally reach dinosaur adulthood, you will gain the ability to lay eggs that hatch into AI-controlled baby dinosaurs. Your babies will grow into adults and stick around for up to half an hour before despawning.

CHICKENENGINEER
When he started out making Dinosaur Simulator, ChickenEngineer just wanted a game where he could play as a dinosaur. It has since evolved into a prehistoric classic! Below, ChickenEngineer talks about secure coding, how to avoid extinction, and if there is life after dinosaurs.

ON SURPRISE SUCCESS
Dinosaur Simulator is a unique mash-up of simulation and survival, but it seems to have found a huge fan base, which was quite a surprise to ChickenEngineer. "I didn't really expect to do well at all," he explains. "It wasn't even a game I intended for that many people to play, and I just wanted to be a dinosaur. What it is now is way beyond my expectations."

ON DINOSAUR SURVIVAL
"It's much easier to play as herbivore and omnivore dinosaurs in Dinosaur Simulator,"

ChickenEngineer informs us. "Most of the time they are faster than the carnivores, and it's much easier to find food around the map to help you to survive longer."

ON A NEW WORLD
So, what's next for ChickenEngineer? Maybe a sequel-saurus? "I'm not sure. I'm always debating if I should do a sequel," he says. "But that would slow down development on the original. I'm currently working on a pet game as a side project, and who knows, maybe that will take off too!"

WORK AT A PIZZA PLACE

Love pizza? Looking for a job? Then make your way down to Builder Brothers Pizza! There's a role for everyone at this popular restaurant, where making pizza is all about teamwork. It's the perfect place to earn a living, make friends, and sample tasty pizzas!

You get to choose your own role at the pizza place from one of five available jobs. Each role has its own tasks, from prepping tasty pizza bases to taking customer orders.

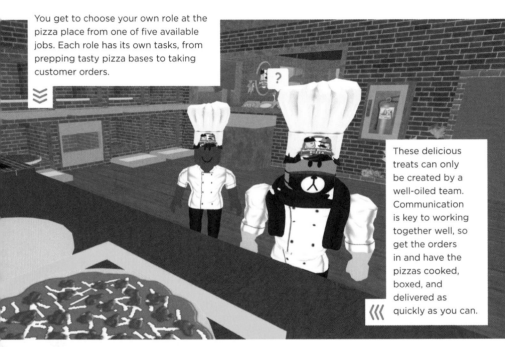

These delicious treats can only be created by a well-oiled team. Communication is key to working together well, so get the orders in and have the pizzas cooked, boxed, and delivered as quickly as you can.

As your pizza creations are delivered, you earn money to spend on your home. You can buy new furniture to create the house of your dreams, decorate it in your favorite style, and even get yourself a pet!

GAME STATS

DEVELOPER: Dued1

SUBGENRES: Town and City, Simulation

VISITS:

FAVORITED:

QUICK TIPS

EXPRESS DELIVERY
To get orders to customers as quickly as possible, grab as many as you can carry, jump in a delivery car, and click on the pizzas in your inventory. Then, just follow the arrow lines that guide you to the customers' homes.

CAREER SWITCH
You don't have to stick to the role you chose if you want to try something new. To change your role, just move to a different area of the store (or the delivery depot) and begin working. Your role will update automatically.

CO-OP MODE
Teamwork is key, so split the duties. If you're making pizzas, one person should assemble while another operates the ovens. If you're on the supply team, have a few people filling trucks while others drive back and forth.

EMPLOYEE POWER
If you think the manager isn't doing a good job, go to the small room near the manager's office. Step on the button inside to vote to remove the manager. Eight employees need to vote for the manager to be fired.

DUED1

All Dued1 ever wanted was to be a self-employed game developer, and after a decade on Roblox, his dream has finally been realized. Here he takes time out from his busy schedule to reveal how walking is the perfect way to get going on an idea, as well as a few hidden secrets from his signature game.

ON WALKING THROUGH AN IDEA
"If you ever want to come up with a ton of ideas for new games, or want to flesh out an existing idea, take a long walk," says Dued1, when asked about his game development methods. "Almost all my ideas come to me while I'm walking and brainstorming. My walks tend to last for a few hours, and I can get very excited when I come up with a new idea!"

ON WORKPLACE SECRETS
Think you've seen everything there is to see at Builder Brothers Pizza? "There's a secret, run-down break room inside the Pizza Place!" he says. "On the outside, next to the drive-through window, there is a darkened wall. Jump into the darker wall and take a break! Also, there's a secret underwater cave near the supply factory."

ON THE ULTIMATE GAME
"My dream Roblox game would be an economy simulation," Dued1 tells us. "Players would be able to buy plots of land and build houses, factories, and businesses where they can live or work. Then other players can find jobs and buy or rent apartments."

ROBLOXIAN HIGHSCHOOL

Whoever said school was boring never attended Robloxian Highschool. Every lesson is filled with exciting activities, the campus is bursting with extracurricular fun, and there are dozens of students to get to know. It's the perfect place for an education. In fact, you might not want to graduate...

When you spawn at the main building, click your avatar icon button to create a new high school persona. Choose new clothes and lots of accessories to look as cool, or as geeky, as you want. You can even pick a new name and give yourself a backstory.

When you enroll, you get to choose which of eight cliques to join, from sporty athletes to stern teachers. As you enter the game, you get a "daily spin" and a chance to win in-game coins that you can spend on gear, furniture, and other cool stuff.

School days are jam-packed full of fun lessons and things to do. Each lesson has a unique minigame to play, from decorating cakes in baking class to mixing exploding potions in chemistry.

GAME STATS

STUDIO:	RedManta LLC
SUBGENRES:	Town and City, Exploration
VISITS:	
FAVORITED:	

QUICK TIPS

SPORTS CLUB
There are plenty of sports to try in Robloxian Highschool. You can play football or volleyball, or go for a few laps in the swimming pool. You can even test your accuracy skills in archery, or work out at the gym!

STYLE ICON
You can spend in-game coins to get vehicles, skateboards, gear, furniture, clothes, and food. You can even buy experiences, like go-karting! Get coins from the daily spin or trade in some of your spare Robux.

HOME FROM HOME
Click on the housing icon in the sidebar to choose a dorm to live in. You can decorate it in an array of colors, and furnish it in any style you want. If you have Robux to spare, you can even throw your own dorm-warming party!

HANGING OUT
One of the most fun activities is hang-gliding. Go to the top of the hill near the school, equip the hang glider, then run and jump off the launchpad. You can glide around the skies and admire the view of the high school below.

SHARKSIE & ABSTRACTALEX

Sharksie and AbstractAlex had so much fun making Robloxian Highschool that they'd go back and do it all over again! They do say your school days are the best of your life! Here, the pair give us the lowdown on game-making homework, how players always surprise them, and some school secrets!

ON TIME TO LEARN
What makes this dev duo super-students of Roblox? "Making a game isn't easy," they reveal. "It's very easy to underestimate the time it takes to make a game, so it's really important to have good time-management skills. Also, it takes time to learn how Roblox Studio works, which is the real secret weapon to making games!"

ON COMMUNITY CREATIONS
"We never dreamt of Robloxian Highschool being so hugely popular," they tell us. After working on hits such as Tiny Tanks and Knife

Capsules, you'd think success would be second nature. "It surprises us how players engage with the game, especially all the crazy UGC outfits our community creates with the Avatar Editor!"

ON SCHOOL RUMORS
You should never believe everything you hear, unless it comes from Sharksie's mouth! "If you flip a switch in the swimming pool area, you can discover a hidden cave," whispers Sharksie. "Also, if you dare to go to the school at night, you may come face-to-face with a ghost that haunts the school halls!"

ADOPT ME!

Be a happy family and hone your parenting skills, or find your inner child and play as a kid in this family-favorite game. Players can form families and explore the world, go on shopping trips, rent a house, then finish the perfect family day out at the park.

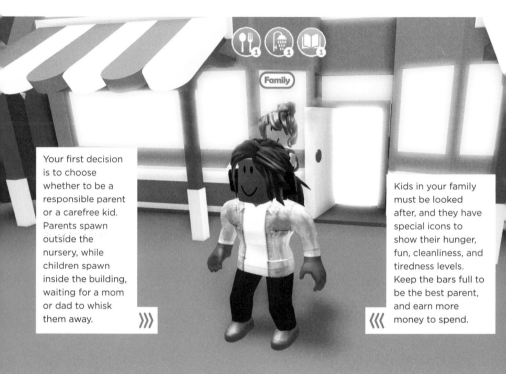

Your first decision is to choose whether to be a responsible parent or a carefree kid. Parents spawn outside the nursery, while children spawn inside the building, waiting for a mom or dad to whisk them away. 》》》

《《《 Kids in your family must be looked after, and they have special icons to show their hunger, fun, cleanliness, and tiredness levels. Keep the bars full to be the best parent, and earn more money to spend.

The world is full of interesting places for family outings. Boost your kids' fun levels at the park, or go for a swim at the pool for some cleanliness points. Then, before you tuck your children in for a good night's sleep, 《《《 treat them to a slice at the pizza parlor!

GAME STATS

STUDIO:	DreamCraft
SUBGENRES:	Town and City, Simulation
VISITS:	
FAVORITED:	

QUICK TIPS

BALLOON RIDE
In the middle of town is a large airship tethered to a hot-air balloon. For five in-game bucks, you can charter the airship for a ride up to Sky Castle. It's the perfect family excursion! But how do you get back down to Robloxia?

DOWN TO EARTH
When you have finished sightseeing at Sky Castle, there's an awesome way to get down – bungee jumping! Enjoy a bouncy trip back to terra firma by stepping off the ledge. Don't worry – it's perfectly safe for people of all ages.

THE HOMESTEAD
You'll need a place for the whole family to live, so make sure to go house-hunting. You can rent an apartment, or a little detached house... or if you have a growing family you might want to upgrade to a stately mansion!

FAMILY RIVALRY
There are lots of different areas to discover around Adopt Me! For some family-friendly competition, head to the park, where you can try out over a dozen different obby courses! Who will win – the parents or the kids?

NEWFISSY

Along with his development partner, Bethink, NewFissy is the brains behind the smash hit Adopt Me! They utilize their love of games and their coding expertise to give their games an innovative design. Here, NewFissy tells us how clean code equals longevity and why the first few months are the hardest.

ON CLEAN CODE
The DreamCraft duo didn't always have the best habits, as NewFissy reveals. "I previously worked on TreeLands, which I took a lot of pride in, but it is now so messy, I can't remember how many parts of the code work! For Adopt Me! I've learned my lesson, and things are clean and tidy, so we can continue to work on it for years to come!"

ON THE "NO GAME" PERIOD
"The first few months on a new project are the hardest," reveals NewFissy, "especially when you don't have a working prototype to show to others. When there's no game, you don't know how it will be received or if it will be fun to play. You start to doubt yourself, especially when your game isn't targeted at your own age range and is for a younger audience, such as Adopt Me!"

ON LARGE FAMILIES
"We've been blown away by the response from Adopt Me! players," reveals NewFissy. The game received over 450 million visits in less than a year. "Our players surprise us all the time, with their gorgeous houses, and how they take care of huge families and play for hundreds of hours!"

BOOGA BOOGA

Are you a born survivor? Could you survive on a desert island with only a rock and your bloxy wits? If you answered in the affirmative to both questions – and have a fondness for wearing leafy vests and pants – then get ready to go back to nature in Booga Booga!

<<< Find materials – like logs, leaves, and stone – to craft items. You'll level up as you collect materials, unlocking more powerful "item recipes." These recipes will allow you to harvest rarer resources.

You can try to survive on your own, or join a tribe. Rival tribes may start clan wars over resources and territory, so make sure you have the best armor and weapons available at your base.

There are lots of unique islands to discover and a range of resources to collect on them. From small desert islands to volcanic peninsulas, the varied landscape means a new challenge each time you play. There's even a secret dimension to explore!

GAME STATS

DEVELOPER: Soybeen
SUBGENRES: Survival, PvP, Crafting
VISITS:
FAVORITED:

QUICK TIPS

COOK OUT
You need to eat food to stay healthy, but be careful what you put in your mouth! Watch out for raw meat and fish. You need to craft a campfire to cook them, otherwise your health will drop with every bite!

DROP-OFF
If you become overloaded with resources, build a chest to store extra materials. Just walk up to your chest and drop the items inside to unburden yourself and allow space so you can collect even more materials and items.

MORE MOJO
Once you reach level 100, you have the chance to "rebirth," which rewards you with a Mojo Point, but starts you from level 1 again. Mojo Points are used to buy amazing abilities and items to help you become a tribal god!

WATCH THE SKY
Look out for unique events that occur around the island, as they can help you get hard-to-find resources. For example, meteors might occasionally fall to Earth and create coveted deposits of the rare magnetite resource!

SOYBEEN

The Booga Booga creator has been on Roblox since 2010. After making lifelong friends in the community of his favorite game, Survival 303, he's slowly been morphing into a renowned developer. Here, he reveals his dev secrets, epic surprises hidden in his game, and how to become a tribal god.

ON GAME DEVELOPMENT
"My secret weapon has always been curiosity. You must experiment and ask questions!" reveals Soybeen. "People love to share what they know. The next step was teaching others, which is a great way to reinforce your knowledge. When it comes to learning, there are no cheat codes!"

ON BIG SURPRISES
Soybeen is surprised how gamers play Booga Booga: "People like to invest massive amounts of time into building cities of epic proportions, even though they know that their empire will be gone once they leave the game. There's something about the transience of what they achieve in the session that makes it memorable."

ON BOOGA BREAD AND EGGS
"The best food sources are wheat and corn, which can be mashed and baked into Bread and Cornbread." He also reveals a couple of Easter eggs hidden in the game: "There's a golden shark that, if you saddle it, becomes the fastest boat in the game. Also, if you try to place a chest on another player to trap them, it will be placed on YOU instead! That'll teach ya!"

FASHION FAMOUS

Have you ever wanted the chance to be a superstar stylist or famous fashionista? Well now you have your chance. Create fabulous ensembles, strut your stuff on the catwalk, and look totally fierce as you try to win the votes of the judges and become the talk of the fashion world.

The aim of this game is to create fabulous outfits that define the theme of each round. Wow the judges (and your stylish opponents) at the runway walk-off to be voted the best-dressed competitor.

The themes of the round are varied and should be followed closely if you want to beat your fellow fashionistas. You have three minutes to dash around the randomized wardrobe area to find the perfect themed outfit.

Although a judging panel greets you at the end-of-round catwalk show, your opposition actually votes on the outfits. Each player gets a chance to walk the walk and strike a pose in an attempt to gain a high star rating.

GAME STATS

STUDIO:	Fashion Famous
SUBGENRES:	Fashion, PvP
VISITS:	
FAVORITED:	

QUICK TIPS

STYLIST'S CHAIR

To finish off the perfect outfit, make your way to the hair salon in the middle of the dressing area. Choose the hairstyle that sets off your look and then use the different blow-dry machines to add the color or pattern you want!

CLOSET MODEL

You might want to get ready without your rivals' prying eyes on you. Create your own walk-in wardrobe by going to the closets at the edge of the dressing area. Now you can stock your private closet with all your fashion faves.

STRIKE A POSE

Choosing the right outfit is only part of the challenge. To really wow your opponents, make use of all the emotes you have as you walk down the runway – point, cheer, and dazzle onlookers with your sweet moves.

PET PERFECT

Win over the catwalk crowd with your very own fashion pet. Think about which animal accessory will match your look and the theme. For instance, a seahorse pet would go perfectly with an awesome aquatic mermaid.

PIXELATEDCANDY

After years of trial and error and learning from others, PixelatedCandy created her masterpiece Fashion Famous. She was blown away at how popular the game was on its release. Here she explains her top design tips, what her fiercest game would be, and how Roblox has changed her life.

ON DESIGNING GAMES

"There is a huge library of valuable information for beginners and experienced developers at the Roblox Developer Hub," says PixelatedCandy. "Also, the most challenging part about starting is actually coming up with the idea. More often than not, the best ideas stem from simple and addictive game mechanics."

ON FASHION LIFE

"My dream game would be a global fashion life sim where players work their way from the bottom to the top of the fashion industry," reveals PixelatedCandy. "The endgame would essentially be for players to grow into A-list celebrities and become truly fashion famous!"

ON NEW FRIENDS

We all know Roblox is social, but for some, its effects are profound. "Roblox has really brought such amazing people into my life," she tells us. "Playing games with friends online, who have now become part of my real life – it's crazy really. Also, I've met people in the community who share my love for fashion, such as Nilvou, Mockeri, Kiouhei, and PRINCE_STARRR."

VEHICLE SIMULATOR

Cruise around the city of Bloxywood and enjoy its quiet city streets... or put the pedal to the metal in high-octane highway racing challenges. Vehicle Simulator is a gearhead's playground, where you can test-drive supercars, compete in drag races, and even fly stunt planes!

As you enter the city limits of Bloxywood, you can choose to cruise around as a speed-loving citizen, or patrol as a ticket-issuing cop.

As a citizen, you start with a cash card that allows you to buy your first car. You may not be able to afford your dream car right away, but you can take it for a 10-minute test drive!

The city has awesome jumps and obstacles that are perfect for spectacular driving. There are circuits and challenges all around the city for some competitive driving as well.

If you're looking for new wheels, there are dealerships all over the city. There's a harbor outlet where you can buy a yacht, and one at the airport, where you can buy a plane!

GAME STATS

DEVELOPERS: Simbuilder, Belzebass, ScriptOn, MarioMan57169

SUBGENRES: Driving, Town and City

VISITS:

FAVORITED:

QUICK TIPS

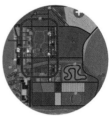

CAR PHONE

As well as a fleet of cars, you also have a cell phone at your disposal, and it will quickly become your favorite item. Use it to spawn any car from your garage, or take a shortcut to the race circuits so you can challenge a friend.

CASH CARD

Miles mean money! You earn cash as you speed around Bloxywood. The faster you go, the quicker your bank balance adds up. You can also earn cash as you ride by winning races at one of the many venues around the city.

GPS

Vehicle Simulator has a detailed city map to prevent you from becoming lost. You can expand it to get a better view of the area, or use it as a GPS to lead you to your destination – just follow the line in the sky once you've picked a destination.

TUNE UP

Drive your favorite car to an auto shop so you can customize it to your liking, including the paint job and accessories like rims and spoilers. You can also modify the engine, or add a turbo charger or an ejector seat!

SIMBUILDER

Simbuilder had high-octane hopes for his passion project, Vehicle Simulator, and loves to see how players socialize and boast about their turbocharged cars! Below, he tells us how to navigate game design, drives us down memory lane, and reveals what's around the next bend!

ON TEAM BUILDING

"Every game has major pillars for why it is successful," explains Simbuilder. "We plan our content and updates to improve these pillars, and divide up the work into sizable chunks and hand them to the team member who has the skills to complete the work. It takes time and effort from lots of people, so people skills are very important."

ON INSPIRATIONS

"My fondest memory was when I was learning how to use BuildV4 by blobbyblob," reveals

Simbuilder. "I then met blobbyblob and Quenty in-game and was invited to join a studio group called Firelight Studios. From that moment on, I was inspired to make great things!"

ON LIMITLESS POSSIBILITIES

So, where is Vehicle Simulator heading? "There are many exciting things in the works," Simbuilder tells us. "We're crafting a new world from the ground up and using new technology that will allow AI NPCs to navigate the world and complete tasks. Also, game modes and car meshes will see massive improvements!"

HOTEL ELEPHANT

Take some time out and jet off for a relaxing break at the Elephant Hotel. Soak up rays around the balcony pool, hit the offshore store, or cruise around on the water – it's your vacation so you can pick your own itinerary! Get ready to kick back, relax, and role-play with your fellow vacationers.

Once you arrive at the Elephant Hotel, you can choose your role – play as a guest, waiter, concierge, sales assistant, or the hotel manager. Enter the lobby and speak with the receptionist to claim a room with a view.

You're on vacation, so explore at your leisure. There's a bar to relax and chat to other sunseekers, or you can ascend to the beauty parlor and gym, where you can try out a new hairstyle or chill in the hot tub!

Try on some new vacation outfits at the offshore store. Browse through an array of tops, T-shirts, shorts, and more! If you have any money after your shopping spree, you can visit the basement casino to play some fun minigames.

GAME STATS

DEVELOPER: pauljkl
SUBGENRES: Simulation, Exploration
VISITS:
FAVORITED:

QUICK TIPS

VACATION MONEY

You earn money in Hotel Elephant simply by spending time at the resort. You'll receive $400 for every three minutes you play. You can spend the free money however you want, which sounds like an amazing vacation!

VACATIONER

There are lots of places around the island that allow you to customize your character. If you search the rocky side of the mountain, you'll find a shack where you can change your character's expression!

ROOM KEY

To give yourself peace of mind while you're enjoying the resort's activities, make sure to keep your room door locked. When it's not locked, any vacationer will be able to enter and surprise you when you return.

TEDDY BEARS

There are a couple of seemingly normal Teddy Bears hidden around the island, each of which opens a secret door. Find both to gain access to a nightclub and a character morph ward, where you can change your avatar's look!

PAULJKL

While creating Hotel Elephant, the resourceful pauljkl found snippets of code to help him overcome the challenges of game creation. Here he takes time off from code-hunting to talk to us about staying on track, a Roblox Mobile surprise, and how some players work industriously at his hotel.

ON MOTIVATION

"I always had issues with motivation. I would start one project and then switch between three or four of them, and end up not wanting to complete any!" reveals pauljkl. "I remedied this bad habit by setting myself goals to achieve each day. I then made steady progress, little and often, which maintained my motivation."

ON GOING MOBILE

"I didn't expect much from Hotel Elephant when I made it," says pauljkl, "and nothing big happened for a while, until Roblox was released on mobile devices and I saw a sudden spike in traffic. That's when I started to see all the glaring bugs in my code. Luckily, the player base helped me out, and also suggested what they wanted to see in the game."

ON FERRY SERVICES

"I was surprised to see some players ferrying people from the main hotel to the floating shop," pauljkl tells us. "As a service they would charge $10 per passenger. The passenger then went to the basement and transferred the fare despite there being no consequence if they didn't!"

PRISON LIFE

Live the life of an orange-jumpsuit-clad inmate serving time for a crime you didn't commit (maybe), or if you have the heart of a hero you can become a guard and keep the prisoners in line. Whatever your choice... choose Prison Life!

Your aim as a prisoner is to find a way out of the complex. There are many possible escape routes; follow a complacent guard through an open door, find an access-all-areas keycard, or crawl through the prison's conveniently sized sewer system.

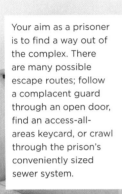

Once you escape prison, make your way to the warehouses on the edge of town. You can spawn cars, pick up some firepower, and meet other criminals on the outside. You now have freedom... but should you use it to wreak havoc or rescue more inmates?

If you choose to play as a "good guy" and join the prison guards, you start in the guards' quarters. Arm yourself with a gun or two for protection, or keep an eye on inmates from the surveillance room.

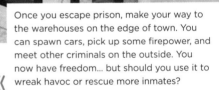

GAME STATS

DEVELOPER:	Aesthetical
SUBGENRES:	Shooter, Exploration, Escape
VISITS:	
FAVORITED:	

QUICK TIPS

BAD COP
When you play as a guard, use your laser electrocutor and handcuffs first and keep your gun holstered. If you get trigger happy and shoot "innocent" inmates, you'll join the orange jumpsuit gang on the other side of the bars.

HAMMER TIME
One way out of the prison is through the sewers, but to get there you need a hammer, and some time on the toilet... so you can bash it to pieces! Once the toilet is destroyed, jump into the sewers below and crawl to freedom!

KEYCARD LOTTO
One way to grab a keycard is to eliminate a prison guard. However, this is a risky move, as there's only a 25% chance that a keycard will drop. Not to mention the guard is fully armed and can easily take you down first.

HANDY CUFFS
Guards can use handcuffs to subdue prisoners, but only if they are not heeding the schedule. So, if you are inciting a revolt, make sure you do it in an area that relates to the time of day. If it's yard time – cause chaos in the yard!

AESTHETICAL

When he started out as a developing noob, Aesthetical admits not knowing how all the features of Roblox worked. He still doesn't, but that hasn't stopped him from becoming the governor of crime capers! Here, he reveals how success surprised him and what's next on his horizon!

ON BEING UNPREPARED
"When I made Prison Life in 2014, I was still a new developer on Roblox," Aesthetical tells us. "Did I want people to play my game and have fun? Of course! But I never expected it to become this popular. In fact, when the game first hit the front page, I was so unprepared that it still had the words 'NOT DONE' in the title!"

ON PLAYING ROBLOX
Aesthetical remembers playing Roblox back in the day with his friends and younger brother. Their game of choice? "Apocalypse Rising!"

reveals Aesthetical. "Getting together to form a group to repair a vehicle, collect awesome loot, and fight zombie hordes was extremely fun!"

ON NEW HORIZONS
Is Aesthetical shackled to Prison Life forever, or will he move on to other games? "Yes, I want to expand my horizons. Focusing on the same game for years can get tiring. I have lots of game ideas. In fact, I worked on a brand-new game while I interned at Roblox during the summer of 2018. I won't forget about Prison Life, but right now I'm focusing on making new games."

NIGHT OF THE WEREWOLF

It's the turn of the century and the industrial revolution is gathering steam, but an ancient beast roams the moonlit alleyways of a town rife with superstition and mistrust. Deduce, survive, and accuse your way to victory in this werewolf mystery, where you need to work as a team to survive!

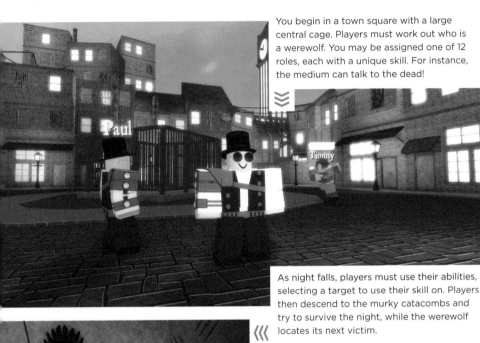

You begin in a town square with a large central cage. Players must work out who is a werewolf. You may be assigned one of 12 roles, each with a unique skill. For instance, the medium can talk to the dead!

As night falls, players must use their abilities, selecting a target to use their skill on. Players then descend to the murky catacombs and try to survive the night, while the werewolf locates its next victim.

As day dawns, a player will have died, and the survivors must discuss, deduce, and then accuse a player who they think is the werewolf. If the werewolf survives unaccused, night comes around again...

GAME STATS

STUDIO:	Sons of Deepak
SUBGENRES:	Horror, Mystery, PvP
VISITS:	
FAVORITED:	

QUICK TIPS

KEEN DETECTIVE
Use your role's special skill carefully to help you deduce which player is the werewolf. It's not always a good idea to reveal your role too early, because the werewolf may target you if they know you have a useful skill.

TALK IT OUT
It's important to talk to other players when you're trying to work out who the werewolf is, but try not to seem too eager to accuse others or reveal too much information about yourself as players may get suspicious of you.

ROLE BOOST
You can purchase a number of spells from the store. Each of the spells increases your chances of being assigned a particular role, which means you can try out new ones, or master your favorite role more quickly.

CATACOMB CASH
While you're exploring the murky catacombs each night, keep your eye out for bright green dollar signs. As you collect them, you get $1 added to your in-game wallet, allowing you to buy more useful items from the town store.

INSANELYLUKE

Even with a decade of Roblox experience, InsanelyLuke still wasn't sure how Robloxians would take to a social deduction game. He had nothing to worry about – everyone loves it! Below, he talks about his first steps on Roblox, a pleasant surprise, and what's next for Sons of Deepak.

ON LEARNING TO SCRIPT
"I started learning to program using scripting tutorials on YouTube," reveals InsanelyLuke. "I also wish I knew how to use Module Scripts when I started out. Looking back at my old code, most of the issues I had with efficiency could have been easily solved with a Module Script."

ON TALKING THINGS THROUGH
"We were all pleasantly surprised by how players interact as they play Night of the Werewolf," InsanelyLuke says. "It's a heavily chat-based game, so we weren't sure what to expect,

especially as some people play with chat turned off. However, players aren't quick to jump to conclusions and jail players who don't talk. They investigate, work together, and figure stuff out."

ON NEW PROJECTS
So, what's next for the team at Sons of Deepak? "We are making plans to update Night of the Werewolf, but all of us are working on new projects. FutureWebsiteOwner is working on Firefighting Simulator, CJ_Oyer and I are working on Pocket Devs," InsanelyLuke tells us, "and finally, LordJurrd is making Island Royale."

THE NORTHERN FRONTIER

Play as a colonist on The Northern Frontier, trading what you can hunt, fish, and mine at shops, or assume the role of a native and craft everything you need. Either way, you'll be fighting hunger and the cold, but the most dangerous thing you'll face will be other players...

(((You begin New World life in the safety of a camp called James Bay. There's a general store, where you can trade items, a bank to store stuff, and a barbershop, where you can alter your appearance.

≫ Outside camp is the wild frontier, where other players can attack you. You can buy a bow, arrows, and a hunting knife to catch rabbits and deer, then sell their skins and meat, or chop trees with an axe and sell the logs.

≫ Buy a fishing pole from the shack so you can catch fish. Craft a campfire to cook your meat and fish and top up your hunger level. You can also craft torches and a blacksmith's station to make even more items.

GAME STATS

DEVELOPER:	FlippinBLEEP
SUBGENRES:	Survival, Exploration
VISITS:	
FAVORITED:	

QUICK TIPS

HEAVY METAL

Try to carry too much and you'll become overloaded, slowing the pace of your movement. Take note of the space (SP) items take up and buy bigger backpacks to raise your weight limit and allow you to hold more loot.

RUN FOR COVER

On the frontier, moving quickly can be the difference between life and death, especially if you're being chased down by other players. You'll walk slower on the snow, so stick to the paths when you need to reach safety fast.

BEAR ARMS

Remember you always need ammo for your guns and bow, which costs money and also adds weight to your packs. Guns also take a long time to reload after each shot, so take aim carefully and time reloads cleverly!

POWER IN NUMBERS

There are many player factions that you can join. Check their description so you understand what they're about. Some factions pride themselves on being unruly outlaws, while others love to cooperate for the good of the colony.

FLIPPINBLEEP

Play The Northern Frontier today and you'll think it was always a super-ambitious game, but creator FlippinBLEEP never thought it would be as popular as it became. Here he explains how that nearly led to disaster, and why playing the faction game is the true test of a frontiersman!

ON ENTERING THE FRONTIER

FlippinBLEEP's top tip for new players is that they should join a public faction before leaving the town. "Players can easily find welcoming factions who will give them some of the most efficient tips to survive!"

ON FAILURE FROM SUCCESS

"It's fair to say that I didn't expect such great success, and it came back to bite me," says FlippinBLEEP about The Northern Frontier's launch. Made as a small community RPG, it wasn't meant to handle heavy traffic. "Some cool

features had to be disabled and later reworked. However, I decided to work continuously on releasing small updates to keep the game going, and I'm certainly satisfied with what it became. I hope our earliest players are still enjoying it."

ON THE FUN OF FACTIONS

FlippinBLEEP added faction customization after release, but he didn't realize it would be so popular. "The game quickly became a very competitive place. Factions are still battling to own areas of the map and a cool gaming culture of its own settled in."

SUPER HERO LIFE I[I]

Throw on a cape and get ready to fight evil in the mini metropolis of Roblox City. This superhero sequel showcases a wealth of genre tropes, including the mild-mannered alias, the secret superhero base, and a ton of heroes and villains to team up with or battle against!

The Lone Archeress

To help you get started, Captain Coolguy gives you the lowdown on everything super and heroic in the game, from changing your supersuit, identity, and powers, to locating your secret base and enlisting for superhero quests.

Combat Mode throws you head-first into danger and battles with other players. Or you could opt for Role-Play Mode, which has all the cool stuff, but without the added peril.

In Combat Mode, you'll battle other players to earn cash, which you can spend on your base. You can also set out on quests to locate artifacts or take down specific players to win rewards. You need to keep an eye on your health and energy points in this mode or you'll be defeated!

GAME STATS

DEVELOPER:	CJ_Oyer
SUBGENRES:	Adventure, Fantasy, PvP
VISITS:	
FAVORITED:	

QUICK TIPS

POWER UP!
Choose your superpowers wisely. You can only have four powers at a time, so depending on your style of play, try to give yourself a movement and defense power, as well as some cool attack moves to fight off villains!

ENERGIZE
Keep a very close eye on your blue energy bar. When it runs down, your superpowers will fail, so if you are in the middle of a fight you'll have to use your human powers to win. If you're flying, you'll begin to fall back to Earth.

MAINFRAME
The superhero database gives you information about your fellow players, including their name, backstory, and alignment to good, bad, or neutral. Use the information to form superhero teams or to target evil foes.

WATER HAZARD
You might feel invulnerable, clearing buildings with a single leap, but like wicked witches and sandcastles, water is your nemesis and you will perish if you land in the vast watery depths that surround the city!

CJ_OYER

When CJ_Oyer made the sequel to his successful Super Hero Life, all he hoped was that it would be more popular than the original. And then it attracted 60 times more players! Here he explains his pride in player creativity, his dream game, and planning for success.

ON SUPER SUITS
"I wouldn't have guessed how much pride and effort people have put into their custom super suits," says CJ_Oyer, who added tools that give players the freedom to decide how their heroes look. "It really shows too. I've seen so many cool concepts for heroes, I've lost track."

ON DREAM GAMES
CJ_Oyer likes the idea of procedural generation, and dreams of making a game that generates minigames. "Then I'd have players vote on the games they like, and the highly rated games

would be put on a list for people to check out. Currently, I'm held back by limitations of time, money, and skill. But if I'm lucky I'll get more and more of all of them."

ON MAKING SUCCESS
The most challenging thing for CJ_Oyer about making games is not knowing whether they'll be successful. "You can have all the signs point toward success and have a game fail," he says. "When that happens all you can do is learn and keep trying, but I dream of the day where every swing I take hits the ball out of the park."

HORSE WORLD

You can live life at a canter, a trot, or whatever pace you like in the equine paradise of Horse World. This horse lovers' playground has a stable, paddock, and racetrack, as well as meadows and mountains to explore, and most importantly, other horse fans to take a trail ride with!

Choose from one of three unique worlds to gallop around, and you'll be taken to the customization screen, where you can choose your horse's breed, color, and much more.

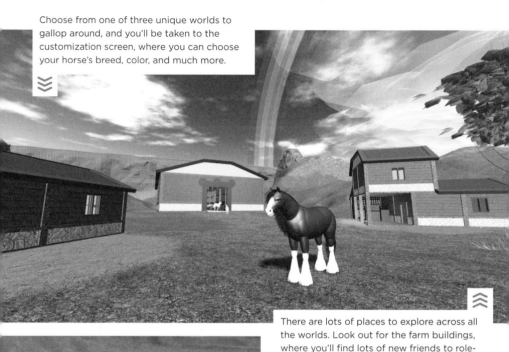

There are lots of places to explore across all the worlds. Look out for the farm buildings, where you'll find lots of new friends to role-play with. The landscapes also have secret areas to find, so trot around every inch and pay attention to your surroundings.

Some worlds also have racetracks, where you can challenge your equine friends to a race, or try out the show-jumping challenge and see if you can clear the "impossible jump"!

GAME STATS

DEVELOPERS: Gangureivu and ExquisiteSereni

SUBGENRES: Simulation, Exploration

VISITS:

FAVORITED:

QUICK TIPS

PRIZE PONY
You earn around $10 every five minutes you spend in Horse World, and you can return to the customization screen to change the look of your steed whenever you want. The more you play, the more unique your horse can become!

WORK HORSE
Your horse can role-play multiple scenarios, from prancing around as a show pony, to thundering along the furlongs as a racehorse. You can even buy a cart in the customization menu and transform into a work horse.

EQUESTRIAN
Players can also explore Horse World as Robloxian humans and interact with the horse characters, adding another dimension to the role-play. Humans can lead around their horse friends or take them on adventures!

TROT OR NOT
Take the role-play experience to the next level with a range of emotes. You can lie down, buck, or eat and drink. You'll also find your speed setting in the emotes menu so you can quicken your pace to match your style!

GANGUREIVU AND EXQUISITESERENITY

Gangureivu and ExquisiteSerenity became friends on Roblox and transformed into an excellent dev duo. Read on to see how collaboration helps them succeed, and how their studio will develop.

ON PARTNERSHIP
Gangureivu tells us: "My biggest secret weapon is ExquisiteSerenity, my partner in development. I see her getting better every month, she is a fast learner." For ExquisiteSerenity, partnership and teamwork are what Roblox is all about: "You get to meet new people and work together in an online world. The Roblox community allows for new and convenient ways to interact."

ON ROBLOX MEMORIES
Gangureivu looks back fondly on playing the pirate classic Tradelands with his friends:

"Traveling was pretty slow, so I told bad pirate jokes to pass the time." Luckily for him, ExquisiteSerenity's memories were a little more studious: "I came home from school, finished my homework, then played Roblox as a reward. The most memorable game was Death Run."

ON FUTURE PROJECTS
"We're making a new game, Farm World, which will take everything we've learned while making Horse World and make it better. But that's all the detail we can give, as it is still in progress. Stay tuned to the group for more announcements."

SORO'S ISLAND

There's nothing better than dining at your favorite restaurant, with delicious food and a couple of Robloxian companions to enjoy the evening with! If this is your idea of a perfect night out, then visit Soro's Island, where the staff are ready to meet all your gastronomic needs.

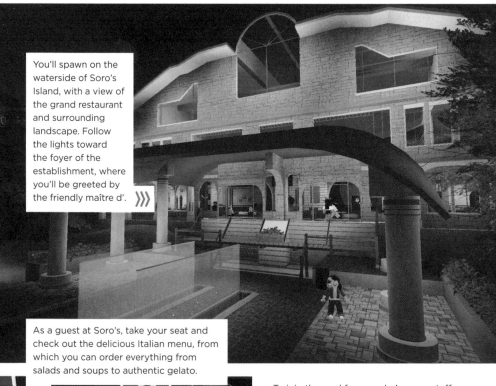

You'll spawn on the waterside of Soro's Island, with a view of the grand restaurant and surrounding landscape. Follow the lights toward the foyer of the establishment, where you'll be greeted by the friendly maître d'. >>>

As a guest at Soro's, take your seat and check out the delicious Italian menu, from which you can order everything from salads and soups to authentic gelato.

To join the workforce and play as a staff member, you need to join the Soro's Restaurant Franchise group, visit the Application Center, and file a form. If you're successful, you'll become a trainee and gain access to the staff areas.

GAME STATS

STUDIO:	Soro's Restaurant Franchise
SUBGENRES:	Town and City, Simulation
VISITS:	
FAVORITED:	

QUICK TIPS

any side orders?

WORKER POINTS

When you play as a staff member, you'll gain Worker Points as you show people to their tables, take orders, and prepare meals. The more points you acquire, the more likely it is that you will be considered for a promotion.

SORO'S TALK

Make sure to talk like a Soro's employee, and welcome people the Soro's way. It can mean a lot of typing, but you can always keep common lines in a text document, then copy and paste into the chat field when it's needed!

TRAINING CAMP

There's a lot to learn when you begin, so Soro's Restaurant Franchise runs a Training Center to help out new employees. Here, the HR department shows trainees all they need to know about becoming a top employee.

DINE WITH A VIEW

Should you want an even finer dining experience, you can purchase a gamepass to dine outside on Soro's decked dining area, or take in the views from the highest point of the restaurant – the grand roof terrace.

INFUSEDTRISTAN

The brain behind Soro's Island, InfusedTristan, immersed himself in Roblox from a young age, with close friendships and cherished experiences all shaping him into the developer he is today. Here, he reveals how to overcome false starts, the great thing about his staff, and why he loves the community.

ON SCRAPPING IDEAS

InfusedTristan always sets his sights high, but sometimes things don't go to plan: "The most challenging part of game dev is taking the time to plan and create an idea in my head, only to discover what I've made is not what I envisioned! It can be difficult to restart work, and harder to scrap it completely, but when it's complete, there's no feeling in the world more fulfilling!"

ON STAFF LOYALTY

"The dedication of my restaurant staff amazes me every day!" reveals InfusedTristan. "The commitment of players to play as a customer, apply to be a staff member, and the effort they put in to work up the ranks and become a high-ranking representative is mind-blowing!"

ON POSITIVE PEOPLE

"My favorite aspect about the community is how positive and genuine people are. They're always there to help when you need them. That's not found in many places," says InfusedTristan. "People of all ages play Roblox, so that depth of experience allows for an infinite amount of knowledge and care across the community."

THE PLAZA

Take a leisurely stroll around The Plaza and lose yourself in a land full of activities, locations, and friends. Take your time to explore the island and you'll unearth a treasure trove that will keep you playing, shopping, dancing, swimming, and even flying, for hours!

The Plaza has plenty of activities to keep you busy! You arrive at the station, from which you can take the train to the boardwalk, or climb the steps to Tower Condos and claim your own home.

Visit the main square to find a nightclub, restaurant, casino, shops, and much more. Farther toward the city limits, there are even more things to discover, including a beach, Ferris wheel, airport, and harbor.

The parlor is home to a few minigames to try out with your friends: Plaza Kartz and Infection. Infection is a zombie infection game, where you try to avoid turning green and clamoring for brains!

GAME STATS

DEVELOPER:	Widgeon
SUBGENRES:	Town and City, Minigames
VISITS:	
FAVORITED:	

QUICK TIPS

Respected

P IS FOR POINTZ
To buy stuff in The Plaza you will need to use Plaza Pointz. You can win these by visiting the risk-free casino, earn them from one of the minigames, or receive them from the hourly or daily bonuses just for visiting The Plaza.

PRIVATE ROOM
Once you've created the perfect condo, you don't want any old Robloxian to skulk around. You can set your condo filters to only allow your friends over to visit. Don't worry though, nobody can move or take any of your furniture!

CITY STANDING
Every visitor to the island receives a rank, which is visible above their heads. The more you play The Plaza, the higher your game rank will become. As you wander around, you'll be able to see who is new, known, or respected.

NOW BOARDING
There are lots of ways to take in the sights of The Plaza, and the best of them by far is from the air! When you have enough Plaza Pointz, you can visit the city's very own airport and charter your own plane to cruise around in!

WIDGEON
Widgeon is one of Roblox's most prolific and longest-serving creators, but despite all his success, his favorite Roblox memory is from when he released his first game and had 20 players all online at once. Here he talks originality, fun, and a big secret in The Plaza!

ON MAKING A DIFFERENCE
Widgeon says success in Roblox comes down to originality. "Create your own technology, like realistic air physics for planes, or custom avatar editors," he recommends. It's a big challenge, but there's help. "The wiki is the best place to get resources," he says. "I constantly use it even after being on the platform for eight years."

ON DEVELOPMENT DILEMMAS
The biggest challenge Widgeon faces is working out how to balance cool features against how well they'll run on devices. "If I want to add a

nuclear bomb with lots of particles, doing such would result in many devices not running well."

ON AESTHETICS
Don't get hung up on how your game looks. "Polish doesn't matter as much as mechanics do. Your game ultimately has to be fun."

ON A BLINKING SECRET
"The lighthouse in The Plaza will flash a Morse code that's unique to the player," Widgeon reveals. "It will unlock an item if they enter that code in the menu." Now you know!

WELCOME TO BLOXBURG

Bloxburg is a friendly town with fantastic opportunities, quaint neighborhoods, and all the local amenities you need to live life, learn skills, and grow as a Bloxburgian! The game is crammed with fantastic features that allow you to create a character, build a home, and play at life.

⟨⟨⟨ You begin with a small house to call home and can interact with lots of items inside, like cooking in the kitchen. Each interaction affects your mood levels, and increases your skill levels.

There's a dozen or so jobs to choose from, including fisherman, woodcutter, cashier, and even janitor. The choice is yours, and you can swap jobs as often as you like.

Each job has tasks to complete, such as styling demanding clients at the salon. Every completed task earns you money. The harder you work, the more chance you have of getting promoted, which means more money to spend!

GAME STATS

DEVELOPER: Coeptus
SUBGENRES: Town and City, Simulation
VISITS:
FAVORITED:

QUICK TIPS

HOME SECURITY
Use the mailbox outside your house to manage the permissions for who is and isn't allowed to pay unexpected visits to your home. You can also give special permission to make other players co-owners or roommates!

TV TIME
Watching TV is a handy way to raise fun and energy levels back to the max. Just sit your character down in front of the square box and watch the mood levels rise back up to 100%. Finally, an excuse to be lazy!

PARTYBURG
You can make good friends with fellow Bloxburgians. The perfect way to expand your social circle is to throw an almighty house party at your humble abode. Will you be the host with the most or a party of one?

CASH MACHINE
You can access the in-game store from the menu in the sidebar, or by interacting with the ATM in town. The store allows you to purchase in-game extras to make Bloxburg an even more welcoming experience.

COEPTUS

When Coeptus started Welcome to Bloxburg in 2014, it was supposed to be a fun side project. It's a little more than that now and has helped sharpen Coeptus' development skills to a razor-sharp point! Here, we discover Coeptus' favorite tools and what the ideal Roblox game would be.

ON FAVORITE RESOURCES
"The Roblox Developer Hub is a great resource!" Coeptus tells us. "I often use it several times a day. It has information about everything on the Roblox platform, as well as examples and tutorials. It's definitely a critical part of game development, whether you're a beginner or not."

ON STARTING OUT
"When I first started out, the most difficult thing was my lack of knowledge," reveals Coeptus. "I sometimes wasn't able to create the things that I had in my mind. Developing games is a constant learning process, so you're always figuring out new ways to do things. Of course, there are things that I'd like to learn in the future, and I hope the process continues to be fun."

ON THE ULTIMATE GAME
"Something I've always wanted to make is a large-scale role-play game, with an enormous world, immersive narratives, and hundreds of hours of content." Coeptus knows it would take a long time, but that isn't a deterrent. "I think the development process would be really interesting, fun, and challenging!"

PICK A SIDE

Have you got a strong outlook on life? Strong enough to wield as a weapon? If so you may be able to use your opinions to your advantage and triumph in the Pick A Side arena. If not, don't worry, in this last-team-standing battle game you also get to use a rolling pin, or a sword!

You arrive in the lobby, where there are two huge screens – one red and one blue. Wait for the theme of the round to appear, read the statements, and pick a side!

Walk toward the statement you agree with to choose a side. Every decision is made in secret, so players will disappear from the arena until the round begins.

The battle arena is a last-team-standing game and players charge, attacking the team with an opposing preference. Some rounds will be evenly matched with equal numbers, and other times you may find yourself alone with just a rolling pin to defend yourself!

GAME STATS

DEVELOPER:	SirMing
SUBGENRES:	Fighting, PvP
VISITS:	
FAVORITED:	

QUICK TIPS

OPINION TWIN

After you've picked a side and battled for your opinions, you can check the menu to see which of the other gamers share your point of view. You might find new friends who share all the same opinions as you... or a new nemesis.

BEATDOWN

You start the game with just a rolling pin at your disposal for arena battles. It's not the best weapon to use in combat, but as you play and earn more money, you will be able to buy other weapons like swords, axes, and bows!

SPECIAL RULES

You can also use your hard-earned cash to activate a special round, which will have its own unique set of rules. This could mean that every player has to use the exact same weapon, or bestow super health on all players.

VERY IMPORTANT

If you've got some spare Robux kicking around, you might want to pick up the VIP gamepass. It will boost your movement speed in the arena, and increase your health, earning potential, and experience points you receive.

SIRMING

SirMing didn't expect Pick A Side, which only took a week to script and another week to polish, to be so popular, but he already knew that a good, simple idea is better than a complicated one. Here he explains why games don't have to be big in order to be fun, and why you should never give up.

ON FUN AND SIZE

When SirMing started out, he worked on some big ideas that didn't work out. "It wasn't until after several failed projects that I realized how important a project scope is. It's much better to start with the core gameplay, and add new stuff successively as you test. I think this increased my chances of actually finishing a game."

ON PERSEVERANCE

Making games isn't easy, as SirMing has found. "The learning curve is high and it takes a long time to be proficient in programming," he says.

There are no guarantees that you'll release successful games once you've learned for a certain amount of time. "I have created so many unpublished games and every time I've thought of quitting. But it's really important to keep trying no matter how many times you fail. You never know when you'll succeed."

ON PLAYER SUGGESTIONS

In Pick A Side you can submit your own questions. "I was so surprised by how good some of the questions submitted by the players were that I added them to the game."

MINING SIMULATOR

Beneath your feet lie untold riches, so why not go digging for them? In Mining Simulator, you'll excavate treasures and invest them in better gear so you can go deeper and grab even more! Find precious fossils, ores, and buried chests, or raise a pet – how far down can you get?

<<< Your mining career begins at a town outside the dig site, where you'll find a shop and a blacksmith, who will buy whatever you excavate. Start by talking to Miner Mike, who'll give you your first quest.

<<< Equip your wooden pickaxe and start digging at the top layer of blocks. Up here, each dirt block contains two dirt, which are each worth one coin. Remember that your backpack can only hold 10 items to begin with.

Sell the dirt and visit the shop to buy a tool that digs faster or a backpack that holds more, then return to the dig site to dig deeper. The deeper you dig, the rarer the items you'll find, which will allow you to upgrade your items even more.

GAME STATS

STUDIO:	Runway Rumble
SUBGENRES:	Tycoon, Exploration
VISITS:	
FAVORITED:	

QUICK TIPS

CUT IT SHORT
When your pack is full, use the shortcut to teleport directly to the shop, then use the shortcut to return to the surface to get back to the dig site. That'll save you time trekking between the two and increase your money faster.

SHOCK AND ORE
Chests immediately reward you with coins, so they don't clog up your backpack. Precious blocks like fossils, pezzottaite, and gold take longer to mine, but they can be sold for even greater rewards, so it's worth it.

DEEP FRIENDSHIP
Follow Miner Mike's quests, and he'll give you an ominous egg. Equip it and go about your mining business, and it'll eventually break open. The hatched pet will boost your abilities, and you can evolve it to raise its benefits further!

COMEBACK KING
Rebirthing yourself means starting all over again. You will lose your coins, tools, and backpacks, but everything you mine will be doubled in value! All is not lost though – you'll keep any pets and cosmetic items.

OBSCUREENTITY

When he started out in the Roblox creation community as a builder, ObscureEntity was nervous about scripting, assuming that it would be too hard for him. It took him three years to realize that he could script himself, and once he finally started, he was hooked!

ON SUDDEN SUCCESS
Before ObscureEntity made Mining Simulator, he made many far less popular games. "I thought Mining Simulator would be a project like the rest," he says, but then he opened it up in beta. "I woke up the next morning to see my game on the front page with over 8,000 players!"

ON THE IMPORTANCE OF UPDATES
ObscureEntity puts a lot of Mining Simulator's success down to continually giving it updates. Why is that so important? "Fans realize how much time I take out of my day to give them

new, exciting, and thrilling content that it makes them more happy to support me, play the game, and buy gamepasses," he says. "Updating frequently really shows the community that the developer really does care about them too!"

ON CARING ABOUT THE COMMUNITY
For ObscureEntity, making sure his community is happy is more challenging than game making. "Without your community, your game won't ever be successful," he warns. He grows it through talking to players on Discord and Twitter, and going into the game with them.

BAKERS VALLEY

Get ready for a bake-off in this fun cooking game, where you can create scrumptious masterpieces that look good enough to eat! Earn money from your culinary prowess, make friends with fellow bakers, and find a little house to call home. Let them eat cake!

The charismatic Uncle Custard will show you the ropes. Once you can mix batter, bake, and decorate, you can start creating a portfolio of culinary treats! You can also work as a cashier and take orders.

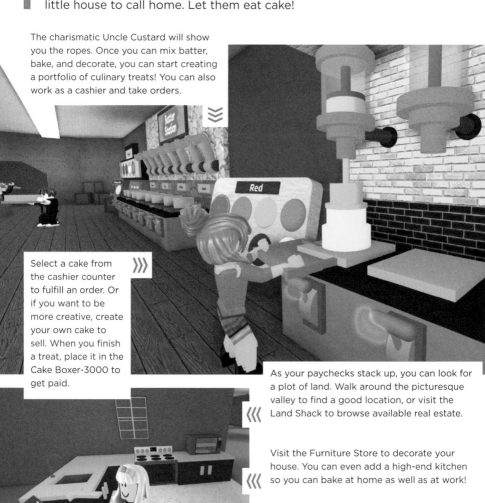

Select a cake from the cashier counter to fulfill an order. Or if you want to be more creative, create your own cake to sell. When you finish a treat, place it in the Cake Boxer-3000 to get paid.

As your paychecks stack up, you can look for a plot of land. Walk around the picturesque valley to find a good location, or visit the Land Shack to browse available real estate.

Visit the Furniture Store to decorate your house. You can even add a high-end kitchen so you can bake at home as well as at work!

GAME STATS

DEVELOPER:	RoyStanford
SUBGENRES:	Simulation, Town and City
VISITS:	
FAVORITED:	

QUICK TIPS

SET OF WHEELS

Bakers Valley is a large place and it is a little boring to travel everywhere by foot. Near the Bakery, Furniture Store, and Land Shack there are car spawning spots, which will give you four wheels to speed around town in. Much quicker!

HOUSE HUNTING

If you buy a house from the Land Shack it may be a little tricky to find on the map at first, so customize its color scheme to make it stand out. Don't worry, once you've found it, you can redecorate it however you want!

TRAIN WELL

If driving a car doesn't quite satisfy your commuting needs, you can buy a maglev train gamepass. The train takes you straight from one end of the map to the other in the blink of an eye so you can sit back and relax!

SIZE MATTERS

The money you earn per cake depends on its size and complexity. If you're not fulfilling an order, add as many tiers as you can and make sure that you add lots of toppings and decoration to maximize your potential earnings.

ROYSTANFORD

When RoyStanford started out, he used to get frustrated a lot, but he realized every mistake was a learning moment and the icing on the top of all that struggle was Bakers Valley! Here, he tells us how he gets in the developing mood, what's happened to Trenton, and how to become a star baker.

ON CODING TO HIS OWN RHYTHM

"I love listening to music when I'm making games," says RoyStanford. "I often listen to soundtracks from my favorite movies and video games." He also has another top tip up his sleeve: "If you do a lot of programming, I suggest changing the script editor color scheme to light text on a dark background. I also recommend changing the font."

ON TRENTON

Who's Trenton, you ask? Well, he's a Robloxian celebrity from RoyStanford's Redwood Prison.

"After his escape from prison he's found a new home in Bakers Valley," reveals RoyStanford. "You can find him yodelling and playing harmonica in a cave somewhere. He makes an appearance in all the games I work on!"

ON BAKING BASICS

So, how do you become a master baker? RoyStanford knows: "Speed is critical when working in a bustling bakery!" he says. "Taking orders also gives you a huge boost in the value of your cake, so practice efficiently creating cakes, then make the ones that customers want!"

ROYALE HIGH

Once upon a semester, Royale High opened its doors to a class of regal learners. Inside its elegant castle campus, there are fairy-tale lessons and activities to transform you from a humble student into a beautiful princess or charming prince. Make sure to claim an amazing dorm first!

Around the campus, you'll find a host of classes, from enchanted art and potions chemistry to magical baking and... English! Each lesson has a minigame to complete, and if you perform well, you'll get top grades!

The Royale High castle campus is too large to explore on foot, so take a flying tour around the school! Double press the jump button and watch your avatar take to the skies as you soar and glide around the world of Royale High!

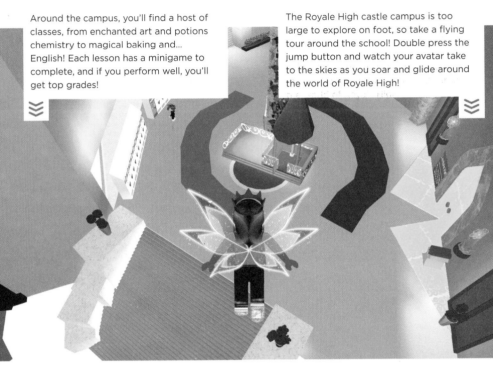

After class, you can dress to impress and dance at the school ball. If you look the part and move with majestic grace, you may get voted the King or Queen of the dance!

GAME STATS

DEVELOPER:	callmehbob
SUBGENRES:	Fantasy, Exploration
VISITS:	
FAVORITED:	

QUICK TIPS

ROYAL LOCKERS
Before each class, you'll need to drop off and collect your textbooks for your next magical lesson. You can even keep all your royal goodies safe inside the locker with a combination lock that only you know the code to.

EXTRA CREDIT
To excel at Royale High, complete your homework on time. You can do it in your dorm, or open your backpack and finish it off between classes. Just make sure you post it in the homework boxes before the final deadline!

STAR STUDENT
Every time you complete a lesson minigame you'll be awarded a grade. The higher the grade you receive, the more your student star will fill up. Once the star is full, you'll earn a bundle of diamonds and gems!

CLASS CROWN
As you ace your classes and collect gems for getting top marks, you'll be able to craft your own crown. You can customize your new royal headpiece and wear it around the school to show off your style and achievements.

CALLMEHBOB

A developer of true royal standing, callmehbob has been reigning over the kingdom of Robloxia for more than ten years. This magical developer's masterpiece, Royale High, was created in 2017 and has grown in popularity ever since, receiving several updates since release.

ON STUDIO TRICKS
"I live by plugins such as 'qCmdUtl' by Quenty and 'Part to Terrain' by Fastcar48, which makes building complicated terrain a breeze," says callmehbob. "Also, I use cones and rings for virtually everything!"

ON THE BIGGEST CHALLENGE
"Update launch day!" reveals callmehbob. "Every other day is a breeze, seeing your imagination become reality is a super-fun process. But 'update day' is by far the most stressful. We test for hours, but it's nothing compared to 30,000+ players playing all at once! They are the experts, and it's great getting feedback on glitches. We appreciate it so much!"

ON A ROYALE FUTURE
So, what's next for Royale High? "Royale University!" callmehbob tells us. "A college campus where you can create your own schedule, earn credits, and study for your dream career! Also on our never-ending bucket list are lots of updates, including a magical PvP game, floofy pets, a mermaid world, and a game where you can create and run a business with friends!"

ACTION!

Team up with fellow filmmakers to create your own movie in Action! Assemble a team of superstars, directors, and technicians to create a celluloid masterpiece. Work together to get the perfect take and make a Roblox movie that rivals the biggest blockbusters!

《《 Only one person per team can be director, two can be technicians, and the other players must be the actors. If you're the director, it's time to write a script and then choose a set from the options.

《《 Technicians will need to select the right effects for the movie. You can control day and night, and create FX like fire and fog for extra drama. Choose the SFX too – you can even upload your own!

Actors to your dressing rooms! Pick out the emotes, accessories, and special costume packages your character will need, then edit your avatar so you look the part. Discuss with the director what you'll be doing in each scene and get ready to roll!

GAME STATS

DEVELOPER:	SirMing
SUBGENRES:	Showcase, Humor
VISITS:	
FAVORITED:	

QUICK TIPS

ROLE REHEARSAL
When you're looking at the accessories, costumes, emotes, and FX, you can preview them on a dummy avatar before you choose to use them. This should give you time to find the perfect items and moves for each scene.

SCREEN PLAY
When you're directing, the script is the best place to fill out the details of the movie you have in mind. Briefly describe the characters and what they'll be doing in each scene so everyone's on the same page.

ENSEMBLE PIECE
Actors have space for expression and improvisation, but should stick closely to the script where possible. If you act wildly away from the script, then your fellow performers might not be able to follow along and play their part well.

BUDGET CUTS
Emotes, costumes, sets, and FX cost money, but luckily you steadily earn it just by playing the game! Directors earn half as quickly as everyone else – the price to pay for the opportunity of getting your vision on the big screen.

SIRMING

Action! was a pet project for SirMing, and it took him a whole year to create. He wanted to make an original game in which players could work together to perform and direct their own films, and that's exactly what he did. How does he feel about the truly unique experience he made? Read on to find out!

ON MAKING ORIGINAL GAMES
Action! was challenging to make because there was nothing like it on Roblox, so SirMing didn't have a reference for what works! "I had to make all design decisions with next to no benchmarking," SirMing explains. "It didn't end up as popular as I hoped, to be honest. I spent over a year on the project, on and off. But I learned a lot that will aid me in future games."

ON CLEVER SCRIPTING
Having made 10 games and with more on the way, SirMing is keeping on top of all his scripting

with module scripts. "Module scripts are cool because I only need to write a function once and it can be reused multiple times," he explains. They're all neatly kept in one place too.

ON SHOOTING WITH FRIENDS
SirMing suggests playing Action! with friends if you want to make a good movie. "It's so much easier to film a serious movie if you're playing with people you know," he says. "It can get pretty frustrating playing as a director with six random players because unlike in real life, you can't fire the actors."

ROBLOXIAN WATERPARK

It's time to don a swimsuit, slap on some sunscreen, and head poolside to Robloxian Waterpark! This sunny resort has everything an adrenaline junkie needs — speedy slides, spectacular viewing platforms, a sauna, and lots of cool gamers to hang out with at the pool.

When you enter the resort, the first thing you need to do is try one of the cool slides. They all start up high, so find the nearest ascending walkway, pick a slide, and jump on!

There are so many slides and platforms to discover at Robloxian Waterpark, so go and explore! As well as the slides, you will find a poolside cafe, lifeguard center, steam room, and sauna.

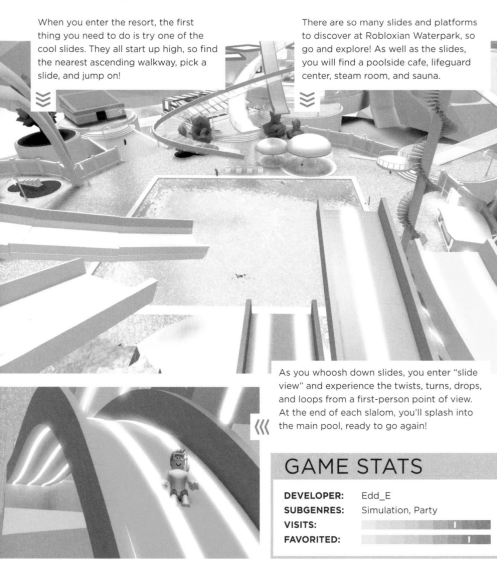

As you whoosh down slides, you enter "slide view" and experience the twists, turns, drops, and loops from a first-person point of view. At the end of each slalom, you'll splash into the main pool, ready to go again!

GAME STATS

DEVELOPER:	Edd_E
SUBGENRES:	Simulation, Party
VISITS:	
FAVORITED:	

QUICK TIPS

SLIDE VIEW

The game shifts into "slide view" when you start going down a slide. But if you find yourself stuck in this first-person view after exiting into the pool, select the eye icon in the bottom left of the screen to switch to normal view!

POOLSIDE

You have all the time in the world at the Robloxian Waterpark, so take it slow and find a lounge chair, then press the pose icon found in the side menu. Select "lie down" or "sit" and embrace looking cool by the pool.

INSTANT SLIDING

Sometimes running around looking for a new slide takes up more time than actually sliding around. Maximize your sliding time by using one of the teleport gates to get transported straight to the top of a random slide.

CHAT 'N' SWIM

You'll notice plenty of NPCs dotted around the aquatic resort, and all of them are more than happy to talk to you. Click on the speech bubbles over their head to find out who they are and what they have to say for themselves.

EDD_E

Developer Edd_E's feet are grounded when it comes to game development. With school, family, friends, and games to balance, he focuses on what is achievable. That's not to say he doesn't want to shoot for the stars though! Read on to find out what drives him, his Roblox faves, and those stars he's aiming for!

ON DEVELOPMENT SECRETS

"While my math, coding knowledge, and other development skills are lacking, my years of experience and motivation to keep learning give me the edge I need to keep going," Edd_E tells us. "You can be the best coder on Roblox, but if you don't have the motivation to start or finish projects, it's impossible to succeed."

ON TABLETOP GAMES

Edd_E loves the instant exposure Places have and how they can be used for more than just games. "When I was younger, I played Dungeons & Dragons with my friends. What Roblox offered us was a place where we could build a map, no coding required, dress our characters, and start an adventure together."

ON SPACE... AND BEYOND

"I would love to make an open-world space exploration game," reveals Edd_E. "My dream would be to create a whole universe to explore, with life-sized planets and randomly generated aliens. You would fly around in your own ship exploring alien megacities and creating your own extraterrestrial colonies."

PIRATE SIMULATOR

It be time to shiver your timbers and weigh anchors as you venture across the high seas! Sail your valiant ship to sun-baked islands to strip them of their riches, embark on daring raids, and gather the cargo you'll need to build a formidable fortress that befits your fearsome reputation!

Welcome to your island! This is where you'll be building up your fortress, but you'll need a ship first. Speak to Jerri, your faithful quartermaster, to claim the Dingy. It's small, but it'll do for now! 》》》

Set sail for the nearest island to mine resources from trees and rocks with your pickaxe. You can only destroy small rocks at the lowest rank, but you earn XP with each swing. Beware of enemy players on 《《《 your voyages!

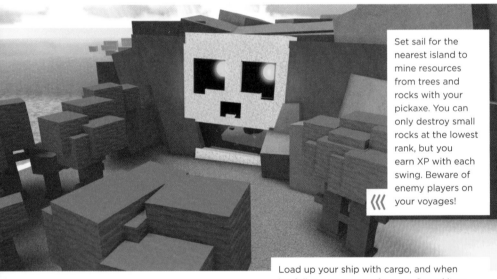

Load up your ship with cargo, and when it's full, return to your fortress. Spend it on defenses such as walls and gateways, which 《《《 will keep raiders from getting to your booty!

GAME STATS

STUDIO:	Explosive Entertainment Studio
SUBGENRES:	Fighting, Naval, Tycoon
VISITS:	
FAVORITED:	

QUICK TIPS

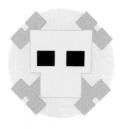

LOAD BEARING
Your ship carries cargo, and you can too! Even if your ship is full to the brim with wares, gather as much plunder as you can before returning to your island to unload. That way, you'll get the most out of each voyage.

MIND THE GAP
When you build your fortress, don't forget to add a gateway as soon as you can. After all, a wall is only as strong as any hole you've left in it! Your walls could reach to the sky but enemies can still walk right through a gateway.

CHART TOPPER
It's easy to wander onto an island and lose your ship, but the green mark on your mini-map will show you exactly where you've left it. Keep your spyglass trained on the red marks, which show where rival vessels are moored.

UNCHARTED
It takes time for resources to regenerate. If you're competing for resources with other players, consider setting a course for quieter islands. They might be farther away, but you'll amass your stash more quickly!

EXPLOD_E

Explod_e started out on Roblox at the age of eight playing games like Lando64000's A Pirate's Life, and now he runs a Roblox game production studio. His goal is to provide the kind of fun experiences he grew up with for a new generation of players, some of whom could be future creators too!

ON THE TROUBLE WITH LAUNCHING
Explod_e says an old programmer joke called "the 90-90 rule" couldn't be more true for his experience of releasing games. "It goes, 'The first 90% of the code accounts for the first 90% of development time. The remaining 10% of the code accounts for the other 90% of the development time.' I've found this throughout all of my releases."

ON A GUILTY SECRET
Sometimes shortcuts can be useful for a Roblox creator, even if other creators frown on them.

"When I'm producing maps and building, Gapfill is a lifesaver. It's a plugin that fills gaps with wedges and parts, and it is so useful when you make a slight mistake!"

ON A DREAM PROJECT
When he was younger, Explod_e imagined making a huge online zombie apocalypse game. "It would still be incredible," he says, but his vision is a while away. "To achieve this kind of game with proper detail would require mapping technologies we simply don't have yet, but it'd be my ideal game. I'm an escapist for sure!"

STYLZ MAKEOVER

Run the salon of your dreams in Stylz Makeover! Invite customers to your station and choose cute haircuts, stunning makeovers, and on-trend outfits for them, then wait for the tips and ratings to flood in. Will you make the salon a super success or will it be a fashion flop?

(((Take your pick of roles at the salon – greet clients at reception, become a stylist and go wild on customers' hairstyles, or become a dresser to customize visitors' outfits.

Visitors will approach you to request your skills. If they like what you do, you'll get a good rating and a nice tip! You'll also earn gems just by working in the salon.)))

You can spend gems on new accessories and styling options to give to your customers, or you could save up to buy a house, or branch out to create your own franchise salon. (((

GAME STATS

STUDIO:	Stylz!
SUBGENRES:	Fashion, Tycoon
VISITS:	
FAVORITED:	

QUICK TIPS

PERKS OF THE JOB
Purchase a perk and you can increase the time limit you have to serve each visitor. This gives you longer to browse the styles on offer and make the perfect selection, or get a bonus on the gems you'll earn from each session.

MANAGING STYLE
One player is assigned as the manager of the salon. They have the ability to give out bonuses, fire lazy workers, and choose the music. Beware: the other players can vote to fire you if you don't manage the place well!

SET AN EXAMPLE
You can style yourself as well as your customers by taking a seat at any of the workstations. If you want to give your clients confidence that you'll make them look great, it's a good idea that you look great too!

PERFECT YOU
You can change your avatar's height, width, and head size to make yourself stand out from the crowd at the salon. Choose preset parameters for kids and teens, or go wild with the plethora of custom appearance options.

RICKYTHEFISHY

From the moment he began collaborating with other players to build bases and plan risky journeys to the Lava Wood in Lumber Tycoon 2, RickyTheFishy has seen Roblox as a place where he can work with others to make great things. Here he explains his delight in player creativity and more!

ON THE BIG PICTURE
To RickyTheFishy, planning is most important. "It may be easy to come up with concepts and ideas, but there are bigger things to take into account," he says. "You have to think about monetization and how to support your game over the long term if you want to be successful!"

ON PLAYER IMAGINATION
RickyTheFishy was surprised and happy to see his players create their own minigames from within his many games, making things he'd never have thought to explore! "It enforces my belief that the best way to engage players is to allow them the liberty to be purely imaginative," he says. "I enjoy giving my players the power to transform their gameplay experience with their own imagination."

ON BEING THE BOSS
Want to buy the best accessories to match your outfit? RickyTheFishy knows the secret: "Earn more gems by working as the manager whenever the role is available to exponentially increase your income, so you can quickly get the deluxe accessory items!"

WOLVES' LIFE 3

Unleash your inner wolf to explore a vast world, make new animal friends, and role-play epic adventures. Wolves' Life 3 is full of tunnels, caves, and volcanoes to discover – there's even a school, a medical center, and, if you want to expand your wolfpack, an adoption center full of eager pups.

As you enter Wolves' Life 3, you can create your lupine avatar. Choose your age, the color of various body parts, and a coat type. If you think your wolf is lacking something, add some cool accessories like backpacks and battle scars. <<<

Once you've designed the perfect wolf, choose a territory to start in, run free across the open landscape, and make some friends. >>>

Talk to other players to make friends and create a pack, then create a den to call your own. There are cool caves around the world <<< that you can claim as your pack's base.

GAME STATS

STUDIO:	Shyfoox studios
SUBGENRES:	Simulation, Exploration
VISITS:	
FAVORITED:	

QUICK TIPS

SIR WOLFINGTON
As well as being able to customize the look of your wolf, you can also give your lupine avatar a fitting name. Select the wolf details icon in the sidebar, find the name field, and let your imagination run wild.

FETCH QUEST
There are lots of items around the world that you can interact with, from balls to bones, and even the odd stick. You can't pick them up with your paws because you need them for walking, so you carry everything in your mouth.

WHOSE DEN?
It's easy for a wolf to get lost in the densely populated world. To help you and your pack find your way back to the den, a handy sign will be hung outside the entrance once you lay claim to one of the spacious caves.

BRIGHT EYES
To aid you in your role-playing adventures, you have the ability to change your wolf's expressions and moods. Choose the emotes icon and pick from a spectrum of moods, or you can just pant like a wolf.

SHYFOOX

Wolves' Life 3 developer Shyfoox loves creating games that tap into the inner child, with a focus on role-play, open storylines, and lots of customization. Here, Shyfoox tells us all about life in the Roblox community, secret tips about life as a wolf, and what's up next for the lupine world.

ON A CREATIVE COMMUNITY
"There is so much creativity and so many amazing new developers every year!" Shyfoox tells us. "I absolutely adore how Roblox gives so much in order to allow us to learn and become even better. Roblox has such a good system of promoting new developers and bringing them into the spotlight."

ON LIFE AS A WOLF
"Have fun! Make up your own story and act it out with others." Shyfoox also lets us in on a special hidden gem in the world of wolves: "There are a few hidden notes around the game. If you find them all you can piece together a story... it's the lore of how the game was formed."

ON UPDATES
Shyfoox gives us some tips on development and info about the next update for Wolves' Life 3, "There was way less stress creating the new update, with many more people helping out, which is a very important part of development... TEAMWORK! It's our best update ever. It'll include so much to do and hopefully some minigames and quests."

PIZZA FACTORY TYCOON

First, you make the pizza. Then you sell the pizza! Then you deliver the pizza. Then you build up your pizza company so it's the best pizza company around! Welcome to Pizza Factory Tycoon, in which you run every part of your dough and topping business for profit and fun!

(((Start your pizza empire by installing a dough maker on your conveyor. As it earns cash, invest in a shaper, as well as tomato sauce, cheese, topping machines, and an oven. Now you're cooking!

Once you've saved enough cash, you can set up shop. Buy the floor first, then unlock the cheese pizza. You'll invest money in building up the restaurant with the red pads, but you'll also need customers (((to expand your menu.

When your first customer comes in, pick up a cheese pizza and give it to them. You'll soon be able to build cup dispensers and milkshake blenders, which will allow you to make shakes and please even more hungry customers.

GAME STATS

DEVELOPER:	Ultraw
SUBGENRES:	Tycoon, Town and City
VISITS:	
FAVORITED:	

QUICK TIPS

STOCK TAKE

While you're waiting for customers to drop in, use the time to prepare items for their orders. Carry a range of milkshakes and pizzas, and get cups ready in the soft drink machine. Whenever you serve an item, make sure to restock.

TAKE OUT

Once you have the phone upgrade, you can take orders from houses in the area and gain lots of happy delivery customers. Take the call, make sure you have all the items for the order, and deliver to the caller's house – pronto!

PLAYTIME

Everybody needs to take a break from work at some point, so make sure you check behind your restaurant. There you'll find dispensers for a variety of crazy toys, from a flying magic carpet to throwable ninja sporks.

TOP COOK

As you build up your pizza factory, you'll unlock the ability to change the name of your culinary establishment. Pick a catchy title that lets visitors know what's so special about your place, and wear your chef's hat with pride!

ULTRAW

Ultraw likes making tycoon games. If he could, he'd make one on the scale of a whole city! But he's still very realistic about the challenges that face every developer, including himself. Here he talks about some of them, but shows that they don't affect his ambitions for the future!

ON POPULARITY

Making games is hard, but ensuring they're popular is even harder! "Games need to be designed so that players find them extremely fun and keep coming back over and over again," he says. "This is something I have yet to master! Some of my games have been instant hits whereas others never become as popular."

ON ORGANIZATION

If Ultraw could go back and do it all again, he would better organize his code! "When I first started developing, I used to create scripts and features that were very messy and inefficient," he admits. "It was very problematic when myself or other scripters were making updates to the game, because we would struggle to fully understand how my old scripts worked."

ON WHAT'S NEXT

Ultraw says his next Roblox project is early in development, but his ambitions are as high as ever. "We have created a very advanced and customizable building system, where players can place their own walls and roofs, and furnish each room in high detail."

ROBLOX HIGH SCHOOL

Your school years are said to be the best years of your life and Roblox High School gives you the chance to enjoy them over and over. So, grab your school bag, skateboard, and, um... fishing rod... and head to the RHS campus for a fun-packed day of education! No, seriously!

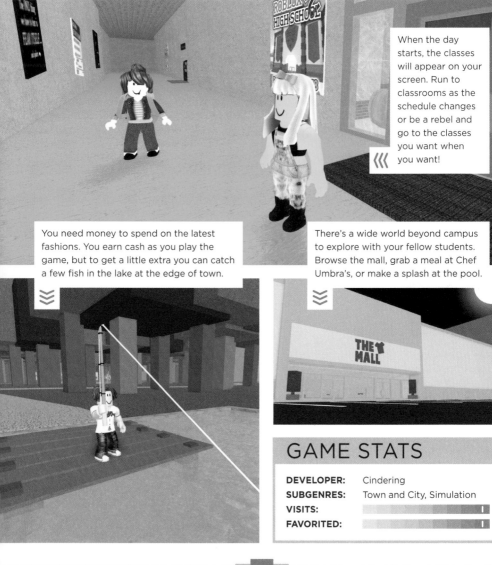

When the day starts, the classes will appear on your screen. Run to classrooms as the schedule changes or be a rebel and go to the classes you want when you want!

You need money to spend on the latest fashions. You earn cash as you play the game, but to get a little extra you can catch a few fish in the lake at the edge of town.

There's a wide world beyond campus to explore with your fellow students. Browse the mall, grab a meal at Chef Umbra's, or make a splash at the pool.

THE MALL

GAME STATS

DEVELOPER:	Cindering
SUBGENRES:	Town and City, Simulation
VISITS:	
FAVORITED:	

QUICK TIPS

MAIN OFFICE

If you're new to RHS and want the lowdown on what to do and where to go, visit the main office near the front entrance. Speak to the receptionist, Brian... who seems to look a lot like developer Cindering in disguise!

DRIVING SCHOOL

Running doesn't always get you to your destination fast enough. If you have a need for speed, you can press the car button in your main menu to spawn a speedy vehicle that you can cruise around the town in.

HOME WORK

Like all good role-playing games, Roblox High School allows you to claim a little part of the world for yourself. You can inhabit everything from snug apartments, a cozy house, or even a creepy cabin in the woods.

HIGH SCHOOL DJ

Ask any cool kid on campus and they'll tell you the place to be is Club Red, where you can party all night long. If you get yourself a DJ gamepass, you can play a rocking set at the club, and get paid for every minute you're on!

CINDERING

When he released Roblox High School back in 2014, Cindering only thought a hundred or so players would walk the school halls before skipping class. How wrong could he be? Here, Cindering looks back at how it all began and reveals the secrets to his success.

ON FIRST STEPS

"Start small! When I first started, I tried creating enormously complex games, but I overwhelmed myself and never got close to completing any," reveals Cindering. "Start out by creating simple stuff, and work your way up. It's really rewarding to release smaller projects, and you also learn new skills and gain much-needed experience to create more advanced stuff in the future!"

ON GAME CHANGES

"Test, test, test!" says Cindering. "Whenever you're developing a new feature, or making changes, always test your game. It's really motivating to see your progress, and it's a lot easier to find bugs, especially if you test changes in small chunks, rather than in big batches."

ON CREATIVE ARCHITECTURE

Cindering was surprised by some players' interior-design skills in Roblox High School. "They found ways to combine items to create something new," he says. "Players only get one-story houses, but some used carpets, cabinets and other items as building blocks to create a second floor and other elaborate structures!"

VENTURELAND

Enter a city built for you and your amazing morphing kart! Race along winding roadways and twisting roller coaster tracks, fly through aerobatic rings, and take part in intense minigames. Then, at the end of the day, relax back at your plush apartment with your friends!

You start on foot, but can spawn your kart at any time. It transforms when you cross water and will grow wings if you launch it into the air. Zoom around the city and collect Blox, Ventureland's unique currency.

You have an apartment in the Tower. Arrange the default bed, tables, windows, and chairs to make it yours, then craft your own furniture and wallpaper using your Blox.

Try different modes, like Destruction Derby, where you smash the scenery, or Bumper Battle, where you push other racers around.

GAME STATS

DEVELOPERS:	SmoothBlockModel, KrixYaz, Wsly, Lunya, EricThePianoGuy
SUBGENRES:	Town and City, Driving
VISITS:	
FAVORITED:	

QUICK TIPS

STARTING LINE

Watch out for the prompts that signal a game is about to start. You'll be instantly teleported to the start pad for the countdown. If you want to play a specific game, select it from the Games tab and wait for players to join.

CITY SLICKERS

The city is peppered with vendors who sell special bodies for your kart's boat and glide modes, so make sure you explore every area carefully. You'll also come across many weird and wonderful characters who inhabit Ventureland.

GET CRAFTY

You can get new kart bodies by crafting loot boxes. Choose the body you want from the menu, and you'll see which loot boxes contain it. Craft the correct loot box to have a chance to acquire the body you want!

BY ANY MEANS

If you're taking part in a racing game, you only have to reach the finish line – how you get there is up to you. Use your boost to gain ground at the start, fly through rings, and hit barrels for extra speed and go your own way!

SMOOTHBLOCKMODEL

The best thing about Roblox for SmoothBlockModel is that it's like a family of creators. When he goes to the annual Roblox Developers Conference, he gets to share tips and tricks about making great games, even with so-called rivals. Here he explains how he learned to develop games on Roblox!

ON LEARNING FROM OTHERS

SmoothBlockModel learned to program with free models and public scripts, which any creator on Roblox can grab, tweak, and use in their games. "I wish I had started using them sooner," he says. "By looking at other people's code, I could see why certain things were happening. I learned all my programming knowledge from Roblox!"

ON LEARNING FROM YOURSELF

"Many times, the things you'll get stuck on will be the things you try to perfect," says SmoothBlockModel. He's a big fan of trial and error, of testing something out and seeing what happens and how the idea can be improved by seeing the execution. "The more you play around with something, the more it grabs your interest. Every iteration means something better!"

ON STYLISH FLYING

Here's a top tip for flying in Ventureland, straight from SmoothBlockModel himself! "You can use manual boost to gain some air in glide mode, but if you toggle into car mode while high in the air, it allows you to do some pretty epic spins and flips!"

FAIRY WORLD

Fly into a magical land where dreams come true! Attend classes at Kingdom High, explore caves and fantastical landscapes, and soar into the clouds. Collect gems so you can buy awesome new fairy wings, wands, and crowns, and then hang out at the disco or by the pool with your fairy pals!

Claim your fairy house in return for a few precious gems. Inside, you'll find it already decked out with some pretty furniture. You can change any item's color for 10 gems, so you can get the exact look you want.

As you explore the magical world, keep an eye out for green gems scattered on the ground and floating in the air, which you can use to buy wands, crowns, and wings. Maybe you'll find a few secrets on your travels too.

If you prefer a routine, there's a schedule of activities that pop up on your screen. The agenda changes every day, from pool parties to study periods at Kingdom High!

GAME STATS

STUDIO:	Sorcerers Supreme
SUBGENRES:	Fantasy, Town and City
VISITS:	
FAVORITED:	

QUICK TIPS

UNDER A SPELL
Join a fairy clan – either Aqua, Fire, or Nature – to gain special powers! Each clan has a different strength and weakness to another clan. Aqua beats Fire, which is strongest against Nature, which in turn trumps Aqua.

TAKE A WING
To fly, double-tap jump and press forward. Every second you fly consumes some of your pixie dust, but you can regain this by landing and resting on land, or by eating food, which gives a quick, sudden boost.

RETAIL THERAPY
Spend the gems you collect on things such as fairy wings, fairy crowns, and magical wands. You can equip the items you have bought from your inventory screen, so you can change your outfit for a number of different occasions.

GOOD LOOKS
Use the Avatar Editor to put on amazing dresses, and extravagant headgear. You can make yourself look like a perfect fairy, or turn yourself into something else entirely – maybe an evil villain for a role-play scenario.

RICKYTHEFISHY
RickyTheFishy feels he can make anything his imagination comes up with, and that's because he works with a network of skilled Roblox developers. For him, it's all about the team! Here he talks about what it means for him to be part of the Roblox community, and his love for the sea.

ON OCEANS
It shouldn't be too much of a surprise, but if RickyTheFishy had unlimited time and skills, he'd make an underwater exploration game. "It would take advantage of Roblox's virtual reality compatibility to let players learn about coral reefs, the animals that inhabit them, and the threats they're facing," he says.

ON PRICELESS WANDS
Just to underline his love for the sea, in Fairy World there's a hidden wand called The Ricky Wand. "It was designed after my personal interest in sharks and emits shark teeth when waved around," says RickyTheFishy, before explaining it's incredibly expensive. "There are currently only three owned in the entire game!"

ON HIS GENERATION
"I'm proud to be a part of a generation of brilliant young adults and kids who are turning their passion for gaming and developing on Roblox into their hobbies, jobs, and careers, all while powering the imagination of millions of players around the world," says RickyTheFishy. "I feel truly special to be a part of it."

TREASURE HUNT SIMULATOR

Treasure Hunt Simulator is all about the thrill of finding treasure-filled chests deep below the ground! Upgrade your digging tool so you can burrow through sand faster and upgrade your backpack so you can carry more loot. The farther down you dig, the greater riches you'll find!

Start by equipping your bucket and selecting a free area of the dig site. Each block at the surface, and the 100 blocks below, is comprised of five sand, and your bucket will dig one sand at a time.

If you find a chest, dig it out! The deeper it is, the more coins it's likely to hold. Don't worry about getting trapped – you can teleport back to the surface. When you have all the sand you can hold, sell it back at ground level!

Buy upgrades when you can afford them. Pets and better shovels will dig more sand per use, and better backpacks hold more sand so you can dig for longer. After the first 100 blocks, each block will hold more sand, so keep your gear upgraded!

GAME STATS

DEVELOPER:	HenryDev
SUBGENRES:	Adventure, Trading, Survival
VISITS:	
FAVORITED:	

QUICK TIPS

UNDERCUT
If other players join you in your hole and they have better equipment, they'll dig faster than you, preventing you from collecting sand. They will also probably reach treasure before you do, so it may be best to relocate.

PRECIOUS
Some chests will give you gems when they're opened. You can spend your stash of gems on crates that hold random cosmetic skins for your shovel and backpack, which in turn make you look like a pro treasure hunter.

CAVE IN
After a while, the dig site will collapse in on itself, resetting the area to how it was before a hole was dug. It means everyone has to start digging again, but not before coins and gems briefly fall from the sky. Grab as many as you can!

NEW HORIZONS
Once you've collected half a million sand, you can access Pirate Island, a whole new place to dig that's filled with even more riches. But it doesn't end there – after 50 million sand, you can get to Dino Island...

HENRYDEV

Roblox has always been about socializing for HenryDev. One of his fondest memories is spending a summer vacation playing and streaming Apocalypse Rising with his friends, and he loves meeting others with similar interests. Here he is to talk teamwork, planning, and educating others.

ON FOUNDING A TEAM
"When I started developing games, I worked alone and the quality of games was very low," HenryDev admits. So he found like-minded developers to collaborate with and his projects went much better. "When you see someone else contributing to the same cause it helps to motivate you."

ON KEEPING A SCHEDULE
When you're making something ambitious, you can lose a lot of enthusiasm, according to HenryDev, so he advises making a schedule.

"It's very useful to give yourself plenty of extra time to make a deadline. That way, you get a motivational boost when you accomplish it. When you get discouraged, a schedule can help to get you back on track."

ON OPEN SOURCE
HenryDev isn't precious about the scripts and tools that go into his game. "My secret weapon is using open-sourced content," he says. He finds things that are close to what he needs, then alters them to fit. "It's a very good technique for beginners," he advises.

ROCITIZENS

In RoCity you can be the RoCitizen that you have always wanted to be! Get a job, earn a bonus, and spend your salary on the important things in life. Work hard and eventually you'll be able to afford a big house and a fast car to make you the envy of all other residents.

To earn money in this life sim you need a job, so drop into one of the many businesses around town. Each job has a basic salary, as well as work-related bonuses, which you earn by completing tasks.

At the bottom of the game screen is a series of icons that denote your hunger, energy, hygiene, fun, and comfort. Each trait is affected by activities in the game, so make sure you're taking actions to keep on top of each one.

Once you have some savings, claim a plot of land and purchase blueprints to build the home of your dreams. You can then decorate and furnish it with everything you need to live life. You can even throw a housewarming party for your new neighbors.

GAME STATS

DEVELOPER:	Firebrand1
SUBGENRES:	Town and City, Simulation
VISITS:	
FAVORITED:	

QUICK TIPS

APPY DAYS

You can use your phone to teleport to your house, or spawn your car, which makes getting around much easier. You can also use the apps to help with cooking new recipes, speaking to friends, and getting updates on your job.

BRAND NEW YOU

Your RoCitizen avatar is completely customizable. You can alter your expression, hair, and skin color and become a different person entirely. Then treat yourself to a new set of clothes and dress in your fave outfits.

TOWNSFOLK

There are several NPCs around town you can interact with who can help you find your way around and figure out what to do. You can also find a help menu by selecting the "?" icon at the bottom of the game window.

EMOTIONAL

RoCitizens is all about role-playing with other gamers. Express yourself without using words by choosing the emotes icon from the menu and selecting from eight different animations, including waving and cheering.

FIREBRAND1

RPG fan and developer superstar Firebrand1 wants to create something that surpasses his own high expectations. Could it be his upcoming resource-gathering game? Only time will tell. In the meantime, he enlightens us on descriptive variables, role-playing, and how to boost your bankroll in RoCitizens.

ON TELLING STORIES

"I envisioned RoCitizens to be more game-like than other life simulators on Roblox," Firebrand1 tells us. "I left out morphs and props, and focused on structure and defined gameplay. But you can't stop players from acting out their own stories. They love to spend time role-playing."

ON ORGANIZED CODE

"I wish I knew how to write code in a way that was easy to read and understand," reveals Firebrand1 as he talks about starting out. "When you go back and update old code it's hard to remember what you were thinking at the time you first wrote it. Descriptive variables, tabbed and organized code, and comments help a lot!"

ON SALARY SECRETS

So, how do you become a top-earning RoCitizen? "Teamwork is key. Team up with other players while you work at most of the jobs. This will help you earn money a lot faster," says Firebrand1. "Also, once you've collected your hard-earned cash, you can go to the bank and invest it to earn even more money, if you don't mind waiting and coming back for it later."

SNOW SHOVELING SIMULATOR

Every day is snow day in Snow Shoveling Simulator. Gather snow, cash it in, invest in better shovels and containers, and before long you'll be ascending Ice Mountain in a snowplow to challenge the Ice King! Who'd have thought clearing your driveway could get so exciting?

You start out with a plastic shovel. You can clear the whiter snow from sidewalks and driveways. Darker snow in the road is too thick for you to shovel at the moment.

When your container is full, sell it to Frosty, who lives in the cave next to the Snow Containers truck. You can run in short bursts to make the process quicker.

Earn bonus cash by completing quests, which task you with ridding a specific house of its snow. When you have enough money, upgrade to a small push shovel, which collects snow as you walk, and a medium bag, which can hold more snow.

GAME STATS

STUDIO:	Virtual Block Studio
SUBGENRES:	Tycoon, Trading, Humor
VISITS:	
FAVORITED:	

QUICK TIPS

LAZY WORKER
If you don't like the quest you've been given because it will take too long or you have to go to a house that's too far away, you can clear it and get another one that's easier to complete or is nearer to your current location.

SNOW BUSINESS
Before you get a vehicle, shovel as much snow as possible from around Frosty's cave. This will mean you can quickly collect and sell snow in the early game, and leave distant snow until you have a speedy vehicle.

SHOVEL SMART
Efficient shoveling is all about picking a clever position. Equip a metal shovel and thermal pad from your inventory, and you'll be able to gather up to four blocks of snow at once if you stand in between four adjacent blocks.

MY PRECIOUS
The blue blocks of snow dotted around the town are diamond ice blocks, which are worth double the snow of a normal block! Make sure you collect presents when they fall into the map too. Every bit of cash helps.

LOTERMAN23

Before he got into making them on Roblox, loterman23 didn't realize how fun and rewarding he'd find developing games. He soon found Roblox's tools and community, which helped him get started, and though he's faced lots of challenges and knows there are more to come, they're just part of the fun!

ON BEING IMPRESSED
When loterman23 returned to Roblox after taking a break for a few years, he was impressed by the new games on offer. "Miner's Haven and Lumber Tycoon 2, those two absolutely blew me away when I came back, and they influenced me to start making my own Roblox games."

ON A PLEASANT SURPRISE
Snow Shoveling Simulator looked like a disaster when it first launched, as it had a major bug. "It went from a failed launch to a front-page game within two days and stayed there for far longer than I thought possible. I'm still not quite sure I believe it!"

ON NAMING
The shovel seller, Jim, is named after loterman23's great-grandfather. "I remember being fascinated by the tools in his garage and it was a perfect fit!" he explains.

ON CHARACTER TRAITS
What made Snow Shoveling Simulator a success? "Determination and consistency," he says. "As boring as that sounds, when mixed together, they become a very powerful tool."

TOP ROBLOX RUNWAY MODEL

Make the most of your sense of style in Top Roblox Runway Model. Take note of the theme, choose an outfit that perfectly expresses it before the countdown ends, then parade in front of the three judges. Can you show off your creative genius and take the catwalk crown?

Rounds start when a category, like "purple" or "summer," is set. Three people are chosen to be the judges, but if you're a model, it's time to hit the fitting room! You have 100 seconds to find the perfect outfit.

In the fitting room, you'll find rows of clothes and accessories with pads in front of them. Stand on them to try on the item and don't forget to change up your hair and headwear!

If you're a judge, you'll wait in the runway room until time is up. Each model gets a chance to parade down the catwalk and the judges rate them out of 10. The points are totalled and the winning model is announced!

GAME STATS

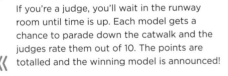

STUDIO:	DizzyPurple
SUBGENRES:	Fashion, PvP
VISITS:	
FAVORITED:	

74

QUICK TIPS

WARDROBE SPY
Watch what the other models are choosing to get inspiration from their outfits, then pick something even better. If all your competitors are wearing fairy wings, maybe try something different to stand out!

LITTLE TOUCHES
When you've won a certain number of rounds, you'll unlock special effects for your outfits like particle trails. Yellow particles are available after just 10 catwalk triumphs, while green ones are available after you gain 70 wins.

WORK THE CROWD
As you strut down the catwalk, use emotes to show off and capture the attention of the judges. Sometimes there will be emotes that play well to the round's theme and really complete the look you're trying to pull off.

FACE IT
Don't forget you can also choose an expression to go with your outfit, ranging from the cute to the crazy! You can even alter the size and shape of your body, so you can fit different outfits to a range of body types.

DIZZYPURPLE

Ask DizzyPurple about the secret behind the success of Top Roblox Runway Model, and he'll say it's all down to making games you want to play yourself. Here he explains how he turned his own interests into learning to make games, and how that led to studying programming in college!

ON MAKING GAMES FOR YOURSELF
"I did not expect anything to come out of it," says DizzyPurple about releasing Top Roblox Runway Model. "I did not make it to get anything in return but made it for myself because I enjoyed it. I have received so many great opportunities because of it and I'm super thankful."

ON ART AND SCIENCE
Making games is a mixture of many different roles, and that's exactly why DizzyPurple enjoys being part of Roblox so much. "I am able to use my artistic mind to create and design things that people enjoy, while also programming, which is my major at university."

ON STUDYING
"I wish I knew how to program earlier on. It really expands your capabilities for making games," says DizzyPurple, who's taken his own advice to heart. "I have been practicing a lot of coding at school so hopefully this will help me write better scripts to create games I could not before. But for now it is all unknown!" We can't wait to see what he learns to make next!

BOOK OF MONSTERS

Engage in a battle of towering monsters versus tiny humans! As a monster, you can deliver crushing blows that will smash buildings and humans alike, but humans are capable of superhuman leaps that can help them reach a monster's weak spot. Will humanity triumph over the monster scourge?

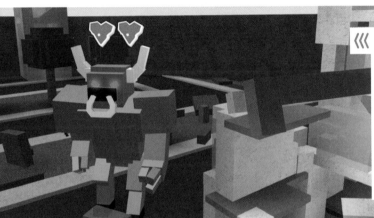

(((There are a multitude of monsters to choose from. Doodleboard shoots a train from its face, Minotaur can pound the ground with its fists, and Casa Loco can start a tornado! Attacks cost energy and need to cool down before you can use them again.

As a human, you must try to jump on the self-destruct buttons on monsters' backs! You have a huge double-jump that can launch you above your target and a dive move that gives you extra maneuverability.)))

Humans and monsters alike have three lives. Use powers wisely to survive the match and take down as many enemies as you can to earn coins. Spend coins on new monsters, costumes, and gadgets that can change your play style.

GAME STATS

STUDIO:	Cosmic Workshop
SUBGENRES:	Fighting, Monster, PvP
VISITS:	
FAVORITED:	

QUICK TIPS

SAFETY FIRST

When monsters spawn, their buttons are shielded by a cover, which humans must first destroy. Once the cover is gone, you can hit the self-destruct button, though each hit gives the monster a moment of invulnerability.

SHARPEST TOOL

Humans might seem to be outmatched by the gigantic monsters, but they have a few tricks up their sleeve. They can equip gadgets that provide certain boosts, and they can use food items to restore energy as it becomes depleted.

HOT TIP

As well as having an arsenal of gadgets and items at their disposal, humans can also explore levels to find coins, in between dodging monster attacks, of course. Collect the coins for a bonus to your monster-slaying income.

FALLING STAR

When you run out of lives during a round, you'll be returned to the lobby above the map. You can aid your preferred side by jumping off the edge of the lobby – you'll turn into a meteor, which you can aim at the remaining fighters!

B_RCODE

If you think the idea for Book of Monsters is strange, creator B_rcode says he'd like to make a game where you fight food monsters by hitting them with your shopping cart... which sounds awesome. Here he talks about being organized, the wonders of bugs, and teaching through pictures.

ON BEING NEAT

Looking back on his earlier games, B_rcode realized he should have kept his codebase more neat and tidy. "I wish I knew how to better organize my projects' architecture, like formatting my code so that I could understand it later. All my old projects were messy, which made them difficult to maintain."

ON TEACHING WITH PICTURES

B_rcode and his team were initially worried about how well younger players would be able to understand how to play Book of Monsters.

"Luckily, we found that many of them easily figured it out thanks to an illustration that is shown at the beginning of a round depicting a human pushing a monster's button, or a monster attacking a human."

ON THE FUN OF GLITCHES

"It's hilarious when bugs occur and completely change the experience," says B_rcode. "In Book of Monsters, there's a bug that happens once in a blue moon that causes everything in the map to bounce; all the buildings, the humans, the monsters – everything!"

NATURAL DISASTER SURVIVAL

It seems like a perfect day on this secluded island – until calamity strikes! In Natural Disaster Survival, you will be facing the worst the natural world has to throw at you. You must use your wits to outlast the storm... or tsunami, or meteor shower, or a dozen other cataclysms.

||| You start on a tower overlooking the map. If a round is in action, watch the chaos play out and await a new one. The game picks a random level and spawns all players in it.

||| Your health persists between rounds, so if you're on your last legs at the end of one, you may not survive long in the next. The Apple item will heal you if you can afford it.

Strategies differ for each disaster. If it's water-based, aim for higher ground. For earthquakes, avoid structures as much as you can, but in blizzards and acid rain, seek shelter. There are many other disasters to avoid, so make sure you have a plan for whatever will hit the island.

GAME STATS

DEVELOPER: Stickmasterluke
SUBGENRES: Survival, Party
VISITS:
FAVORITED:

QUICK TIPS

FOLLOW THE HERD
Other players, particularly those who have played a lot, often have a good idea of how to stay alive on each map, so it's a smart idea to go where they go. But they're not always right! Use your common sense too.

WATCH THE SKIES
When the round starts, you may get an idea of what disaster is heading your way and give you a chance to prepare accordingly. Clouds and howling wind will often mean either a sandstorm or a blizzard is about to strike.

HIGH CHANCE
It's natural to consider higher ground in order to avoid the disaster, but it's often not the best idea. Remember that falling will kill you, so you can't just jump off a tower if it's shaking in an epic earthquake!

CALL COLLECT
There are lots of badges to achieve, which can give an extra challenge during rounds, like getting inside a helicopter in a storm! Find the full list on the Natural Disaster Survival game page to get some inspiration.

STICKMASTERLUKE

Stickmasterluke is one of Roblox's most successful developers. He was the first to reach 10 million visits, and many of them came from Natural Disaster Survival. Why's it so popular? He thinks it's because other people love watching buildings get destroyed by meteors and tornadoes as much as he does!

ON SIMPLE BEGINNINGS
Stickmasterluke advises that new developers start their projects by sketching out their ideas. "Use blocks to represent parts of the game," he says. "Fill in the detail later." That means they can make things quickly and soon find whether they're fun. "And it is okay to fail!" he adds.

ON HIS MAIN LIMITATION
Ideas are easy, says Stickmasterluke. "My real limitation is time. I have nearly a hundred game ideas written down in notepads. Without a time limitation, I'd love to bring them all to life."

ON ROBLOX PLAYERS
Stickmasterluke's favorite thing about the Roblox community is the people that comprise it. "People play my creations," he says. "Not only do they enjoy my work, but they are creative and want to add onto it. So many ideas come from the players. They make my games just as much as I do."

ON HOW TO SURVIVE
Here's a hot tip from Stickmasterluke: "The green balloon is not only fun to use, but is also the best tool to get to save you from disasters."

TRADE HANGOUT

You may be sitting on a fortune in your Roblox inventory! Trade Hangout is a place where you can find trades for rare and special Roblox items with other players and negotiate before finalizing deals on the Roblox website. This is the game where you can make big Robux!

Trade Hangout is exactly what its name suggests: a hub of 50 players, all there to find buyers and sellers for their items. Use Chat to say what you're looking for or what you have to offer.

Select a player to bring up a window that shows all the items they own. You can also put ads up to attract attention and get a list of all the owners of a certain item you're looking for.

Your RAP is the value of your items based on their Recent Average Price – an item's value over the past month. The higher your RAP, the more respect you'll attract.

GAME STATS

DEVELOPER:	Merely
SUBGENRES:	Trading, Showcase
VISITS:	
FAVORITED:	

QUICK TIPS

SAFETY FIRST
Watch out for scammers when you're trading! Ignore anyone that offers "free Robux" or trades with too many items. Check the value of items by looking them up on the Roblox website and finding the going rate.

JOINING UP
You'll need to have a Builders Club membership to trade items in Roblox. Any will do, but don't forget that they all give you varying amounts of daily Robux, which will come in handy as you stock up on items to trade!

SHORT SUPPLY
Only a set number of Limited items exist and there are two types. Limited items were initially offered for sale to anyone over a restricted period of time, while only a certain number of Limited U items were ever released.

DO THE DEAL
When you have finalized the details of a swap in Trade Hangout, go to the player's profile on the Roblox website. Click on the "..." icon at the top and select Trade Items, then add the items you agreed to trade and wait for a response.

MERELY
When he launched it, creator Merely was surprised to find Trade Hangout becoming so popular since it had so little content. But he was in the right place at the right time: Roblox's trading system had just been added and Trade Hangout was just what players were looking to play!

ON REAL WORLD INSPIRATION
Merely is fascinated by architecture and collects pictures of buildings for ideas. "Most of the buildings in Trade Hangout are based on actual buildings around the world," he reveals. "The entire map's layout is based on a beautiful outdoor European plaza."

ON THINKING SMALL
"When working on a new game, make a basic version that works and ask others to playtest it," advises Merely. It's a good way to test core ideas and see if they're worth expanding into a full game. "Not every game is going to succeed, but each one will help you develop your skills. View failed games as stepping stones to success!"

ON DREAMING BIG
If money and skills were no obstacle, Merely has a big idea. "A seamless, persistent, massively multiplayer game where players team up to form their own armies," he says. It'd even be set on a 1:1 scale replica of Earth, made using real topographical data! "Players would be able to take over swaths of land, build defenses, collect resources, and compete for global domination."

VET SIMULATOR

Lend a paw to your sick animal friends and use an array of contraptions to make them healthy again in Vet Simulator. No matter which animal passes through the clinic doors, you and your friendly team can diagnose and treat them, sending them back to their loving homes.

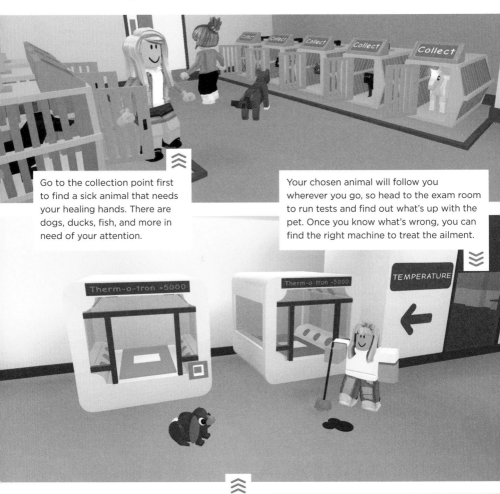

Go to the collection point first to find a sick animal that needs your healing hands. There are dogs, ducks, fish, and more in need of your attention.

Your chosen animal will follow you wherever you go, so head to the exam room to run tests and find out what's up with the pet. Once you know what's wrong, you can find the right machine to treat the ailment.

When you fully treat an animal, you'll receive Vet Points. Take them to the reception area to send the healthy animal home and repeat the process. You can also opt for another role at the clinic, like cleaner or cafe staff.

GAME STATS

STUDIO:	Block Evolution Studios
SUBGENRES:	Tycoon, Simulation
VISITS:	
FAVORITED:	

QUICK TIPS

PET SHOPPING
You can use Vet Points to buy items from the shop next to the clinic. Add one of the various trails so everyone can see you rushing around to help the animals. If sanitation is your game, you can also upgrade your mop!

ANIMAL AILMENTS
Though animals range from dogs and fish to turtles and unicorns, their illnesses are measured on similar scales – hunger, temperature, weight, thirst, sickness, and energy. Find the right way to treat them all.

QUICK COMMUTE
Just beyond the clinic area, there's a neighborhood ready for you and your fellow animal lovers to move into and call home. Claim a house of your own, then gather around the campfire or try to complete the treehouse obby.

TEAM MEMBER
Being a vet is all well and good, but it takes a larger staff to keep the clinic running. Become a cleaner to mop up animal mess from the floors, keep the place safe as a security guard, or serve up meals as one of the cafe staff.

BLOCKFACEBOB

In the eight years since Blockfacebob started to make games, he's learned lots of skills which, as an official mentor, he now passes on to a new generation of Roblox creators! Here he explains the secret of his developing success and his surprise at how players play with Vet Simulator's animals.

ON BIG PLANS
Some Roblox developers attribute their success to dedication and hard work. Blockfacebob puts it down to his big whiteboard! "It's brilliant for the planning and annotating of systems and maps," he explains. "This is especially great when you work with others as a studio. It allows you to quickly explain ideas."

ON GLOBAL THINKING
"Making sure a game can be enjoyed by every player in our target audience is something we spend a lot of time on," says Blockfacebob, who doesn't only think about fellow English speakers. "For example, we have a Spanish translator on the team who helps us expand and grow our target audience."

ON VIRTUAL PET OWNERS
Blockfacebob was very surprised to see how players care for their furry patients. "They form emotional connections, almost as if they were real animals," he says. "I have witnessed people naming their animals and pretending they are actually their pets." With such a range of cute animals, it's no wonder!

RESTAURANT TYCOON

You'll find life in the food trade runs at high speed in Restaurant Tycoon, in which you run your own eatery. Design the menu and layout, then take orders and cook! Eventually you'll be able to hire staff to run the show for you, then lie back and watch the profits roll in!

Open your restaurant by choosing a plot of land, building design, and cuisine. Place two tables inside, with four chairs at each one, and place the counter where you'll cook the food.

When customers come in, seat them at a free table. Take orders as each customer is ready, then follow the directions in the kitchen to cook their meals, before serving to the correct customer.

Be prompt with the check when customers are finished – you might even get a tip. Once you have enough money, hire waiters and chefs to help you, upgrade tables and counters, and expand your premises. You're on your way to founding a food empire!

GAME STATS

DEVELOPER:	Ultraw
SUBGENRES:	Simulation, Tycoon
VISITS:	
FAVORITED:	

QUICK TIPS

FLOOR PLAN
Make it easier for your wait staff and customers to get around. Place the kitchen, tables, and equipment close by so the travel time between them is almost zero. The quicker you can serve, the more money you'll earn!

FOOD SCORE
Your restaurant's rating is displayed outside for all passersby to see. It details your rating for service speed, design, menu variety, and entertainment. Use it to help you decide what you should upgrade next.

GET INVOLVED
If your waitstaff aren't moving very fast, you can step in to keep things moving efficiently. Take customer orders and payments quickly so that you can seat newcomers who have been lining up to sample your food.

STAFF BENEFITS
You can have up to six waiters and they can be upgraded to make them speedier. You can have 12 chefs, each of which specializes in a different cuisine. Once you have a drinks bar, you can also employ baristas to serve customers.

ULTRAW

Even though the Roblox front page can be a very competitive place for a developer, Ultraw says that everyone he meets is willing to help him along. That's his favorite thing about the community. Read on for the secret to his success and what surprises him most about his players.

ON STAYING ON TARGET
Ultraw thinks he's successful because of one particular skill: "The ability to stay focused on just one project without quitting halfway through or getting distracted." After all, you can't release a game if you don't finish making it!

ON EVERY FLAVOR
Ultraw was surprised and pleased to find players don't restrict their restaurants to just one cuisine. "People hire every type of chef, unlock every type of music, and try to serve every single recipe in the game," he says.

ON GETTING RICH QUICK
"One tip for Restaurant Tycoon is to buy as many tables and chairs as possible, and don't worry about purchasing the most expensive and high-quality furniture," advises Ultraw. "Getting a lot of customers in your restaurant will help you start earning money quickly."

ON THE MIDDLE GROUND
Another tip from Ultraw is to put the chefs near the center of your restaurant. "This can improve your service speed a lot because it means waiters don't have to walk far to the kitchen!"

BUILD A BOAT FOR TREASURE

Can you design a boat that can cross the world's most treacherous seas? Create a craft capable of surviving storms, cannon-fire, and water geysers; the farther you get, the more gold you earn. Invest in more blocks and you'll be able to build better boats and team up with your friends!

You start with just six wooden blocks. Connect them together on the grass next to your base using the build tool, and put the seat on top. Jump on and launch!

Your boat automatically sails out to sea. As it crashes into rocks, the weak wood blocks get destroyed, so your voyage won't last long and you'll sink in the water.

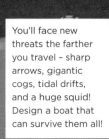

You'll face new threats the farther you travel – sharp arrows, gigantic cogs, tidal drifts, and a huge squid! Design a boat that can survive them all!

Use gold earned on your maiden voyage to buy the most expensive chest you can afford! It'll contain a selection of new blocks that could strengthen your boat, like metal and marble. Design a new boat with your new blocks to survive for longer.

GAME STATS

STUDIO: Chillz Studios
SUBGENRES: Survival, Crafting, Naval
VISITS:
FAVORITED:

QUICK TIPS

FACE FRONT
To begin with, your seacraft won't be comprised of many blocks. Watch how the spurs of land turn your boat around, and make sure the strongest part of your boat tends to face forward so it takes the brunt!

BROADSIDE
When you buy a cannon and place it on your boat, you'll gain the ability to shoot and destroy obstacles before you sail into them. Be aware that large rocks and other obstacles may take more than one hit. Fire at will!

SMALL TARGET
A wide ship will be more prone to hitting obstacles, so consider building a narrow but high boat instead. However, there are still some hazards that can capsize such a boat – tall ships can tip over much more easily.

MEGA CUBE
You increase the durability of your ship by creating multiblocks. Place the same blocks next to each other to create a much stronger variant! Different blocks allow a different range of combos so try them all.

CHILLTHRILL709
Sometimes the best ideas come out of making things for fun, like Build a Boat for Treasure. Having created it simply as a place to play around in with friends, chillthrill709 never imagined so many people would enjoy it. However, the success of the game sent him on a development voyage.

ON HOW PLAYERS SURPRISE HIM
One of chillthrill709's greatest inspirations is seeing what players make. "I remember watching someone load their boat and it blew me away," he says. "I thought, I'm the guy who created this game, yet players build things that look more amazing than the world they build them in."

ON THINKING AHEAD
Even experienced creators can find their projects losing their way. "I have many unfinished projects and I know a lot of friends do too," chillthrill709 says. "I would rush into developing a game, and sooner or later I'd find myself wondering what to do next." But he realized careful planning can point the way, avoiding ambitious ideas that involve building hundreds of items or lots of maps. "I think I've learned from my mistakes since then."

ON USING WHAT'S AVAILABLE
chillthrill709 says translating unique ideas into games is a huge challenge. "I have to admit that I have grabbed graphics provided to anyone for free." But free, he says, comes with a cost. "They never fit well and usually miss a feeling of unity."

THE NEIGHBORHOOD OF ROBLOXIA

Welcome to The Neighborhood of Robloxia, where you can get the perfect job, find an idyllic home, and hang out with your friends. This tranquil community boasts everything a thriving town needs: a school, a hospital, a brave police force, focused firefighters, and lots of restaurants!

You can assume one of 19 different jobs in the neighborhood – from cop to adoption agent to restaurateur. There are some cool places to explore and your role can affect the way you interact with these places, as well as other Robloxian citizens.

Travel to the middle of the map and find a place to call home. Once you've made your purchase, you can buy furniture, decorate the multitude of rooms, and park a car on your spacious driveway.

You can upgrade your estate to an exquisite stately home with the mansion game pass. With more space to decorate, you can create the perfect pad to entertain your neighbors.

GAME STATS

DEVELOPER:	Q_Q
SUBGENRES:	Town and City, Simulation
VISITS:	
FAVORITED:	

QUICK TIPS

PAYCHECK
Each job has an hourly pay, which differs depending on your chosen career. You can use the currency, Robingles, to upgrade your house, or treat your neighbors to some fine dining at a posh restaurant.

DRIVE TIME
Your car is your ticket to freedom around town. You can even change the paint job before you take it for a spin. If you buy a flashy limousine, remember to lock the doors, otherwise it might not stay where you left it!

PET PERKS
Why not experience life through the eyes of an animal friend? As well as playing as human characters, you can use morphs to play as a dog, a cat, or even a bird. Play nicely with the humans and one of them may want to make you their pet!

RPD
As a police officer, use your handcuffs and pistol to catch the criminals of the neighborhood. Make sure you only arrest players from the criminal team! You can also choose to be a SWAT officer and help protect the peace of Robloxia!

Q_Q

When Q_Q first started out, he was easily distracted by small details, and neglected core gameplay. Luckily for us, he found a balance between the two and with it a Neighborhood to be proud of! Here, Q_Q tells us about his dream game, how to avoid bumps in the road, and what's next for the 'hood.

ON A VIRTUAL DREAM
Q_Q tells us about his ultimate game idea. "I am a huge VR enthusiast, so the dream game that I would love to make is definitely one that uses virtual reality," says Q_Q. "Now that Roblox has incorporated VR onto their platform, I can't wait to experiment with all the new tools to see what I can create!"

ON GETTING STUMPED
"I consult the Developer Hub and forums if I get stumped on a particular topic," reveals Q_Q. "It helps to get a good refresher from time to time

to tackle any challenges. I always appreciate the support and enthusiasm from the developer community."

ON UPDATING THE 'HOOD
So, what's around the bend for Neighborhood of Robloxia? "I plan to deliver more activities and jobs within the game that users can interact with, and hopefully it will boost the game's overall social aspect," Q_Q tells us. "In the meantime, I've hidden four 8-bit-style Easter eggs around the game. Click on them all and you'll get something special!"

ACHIEVEMENT CHECKLIST

You've assumed guises of different characters and even different species, but now you must embrace the mantle of master badge-hunter. Below is a list of the most interesting badges from the featured games and how to get your hands on them. Can you complete them all?

1 BILLION VISITS TROPHY
MEEPCITY
Sorry, you can't get this badge if you don't already have it. If you do have it, you're in an exclusive club. Well, not that exclusive, as it was given to all who visited MeepCity to celebrate being the first game to achieve 1 billion visits!

SURVIVE 10 DAYS [CARNIVORE]
DINOSAUR SIMULATOR
Being a dinosaur is easy when you can eat the plentiful plant life growing around the world. For a real challenge, try to last for 10 days as a meat-eater, unable to satisfy your hunger on vegetation. Sharpen your claws...

EAGLE EYE
ROBLOXIAN HIGHSCHOOL
Take time out of your day to hone your archery abilities. It's not as easy as that, though – you'll need to score over 90 points to attain this badge. Hold your breath and aim for the bull's-eye.

1ST PLACE!
FASHION FAMOUS
Your objective for winning this badge sounds simple – all you have to do is win a single round of the runaway runway hit – but it's easier said than done. Wait for your favorite category, then strut your stuff!

NEW SHERIFF IN TOWN
VEHICLE SIMULATOR
Choose a life of crime-fighting by becoming a police officer in Vehicle Simulator. You'd think this would be easy, but less than a third of visitors have chosen to enforce the city's laws. It's a wonder it's still standing!

WEREWOLF VICTORY
NIGHT OF THE WEREWOLF
Howl at the moon and release the werewolf to win this achievement. You must eliminate all the other townspeople before they can put you in jail, but you will have the aid of your werewolf brethren to help out.

MEET THE CREATOR
SUPER HERO LIFE II
As if fulfilling your dream of becoming a superhero isn't enough, you can also meet the man who made it happen. For this badge, you just need to cross paths with CJ_Oyer in Super Hero Life II. Only a handful of people ever have...

JACKPOT!
THE PLAZA
Add a considerable amount to your Plaza Pointz by hitting the jackpot at the casino. You'll need a lot of time, patience, and Plaza Pointz to reach this feat, but you'll have a ridiculous amount of riches after!

DISCOVER UNOBTAINIUM
MINING SIMULATOR
Defy the name of this scarce mineral by actually obtaining some unobtainium from your mining endeavors. It's one of the rarest materials you'll find in the game, so you might have to rebirth a few times before you see it.

BAKED A CAKE AT THE BAKERY
ROYALE HIGH
There are more magical endeavors to occupy yourself with at Royale High, but who doesn't love cake? Take a baking class at Enchantix High and exit with a tray of delicious treats to share with your dormmates.

YOU PLAYED WOLVES' LIFE 3
WOLVES' LIFE 3
This one couldn't be any easier. All you need to do is launch Wolves' Life 3 and you'll achieve this badge. But will you stop there? Probably not – there's a lot of world to explore and plenty of lupine friends to make!

PIZZA FACTORY TYCOON
PIZZA FACTORY TYCOON
All you need to do to easily bolster your burgeoning badge collection is play a game of Pizza Factory Tycoon. However, it'll be a lot harder to put the game down again once you start building your empire!

TO THE MINES
ROBLOX HIGH SCHOOL
School days can sometimes be a little bit boring, so play hooky from RHS for the day to try and achieve this badge. Search around the town to find a secret portal that will take you to Cindering's Sharpshooter Mines.

VALEDICTORIAN
ROBLOX HIGH SCHOOL
This one could take you a while to complete. Spend 3 whole days – that's 72 whole hours – playing Roblox High School. At least you'll be able to learn something as you play... or polish your skateboarding skills on the half-pipe.

KINGDOM HIGH
FAIRY WORLD
Take some time out from the magical activities throughout Fairy World to attend school. Yes, really. Don't worry though, Kingdom High is nothing like the school you know and is packed with magical classes to enjoy!

10B SAND DUG
TREASURE HUNT SIMULATOR
You'll be the talk of the island if you manage to attain this epic badge. Fill your bucket with sand 10 BILLION times to add it to your collection, but beware, there might not be any island left once you're done.

EGYPT EXHIBIT
ROCITIZENS
Another badge that is sadly unattainable now, but you can marvel at users who do have it. This was given to players who managed to complete a tricky puzzle during the Around the World event in 2016.

COWABUNGA!
SNOW SHOVELING SIMULATOR
Get some serious air while you attempt to unlock this achievement. First get your hands on a snowmobile, then take it to the top of the ice mountain. Begin your descent and aim for the ramp at the bottom. Next step: FLY!

TUTORIAL CONQUERER
BOOK OF MONSTERS
Learn the ropes of an awesome game and land an achievement badge? Sign me up! All you need to do is complete Book of Monsters' tutorial to receive the reward... and learn to control giant wrecking monsters.

SURVIVE POWER 7 MULTI-DISASTER
NATURAL DISASTER SURVIVAL
Become the most accomplished of disaster masters by enduring a level 7 multi-disaster – that's seven different cataclysms heading your way at the same time. You'll need a plan, epic disaster-dodging skills, and good fortune.

1,000 VET POINTS
VET SIMULATOR
Master the art of healing animals and achieve 1,000 Vet Points to attain this benevolent badge. Just over 1,000 animal lovers have been able to land this achievement, so it's a pretty exclusive club so far.

EUROPE
RESTAURANT TYCOON
Conquer the culinary arts of the European continent by mastering either Greek, Italian, or British cuisine. To achieve this badge, you'll need to reach level 3 or above in your chosen style of food.

25K REBIRTHS
TREASURE HUNT SIMULATOR
Finally, we have an achievement that will truly set your badge collection above all others. If you rebirth 25,000 times in Treasure Hunt Simulator, you'll earn this ultra-rare badge, which nobody has ever achieved!

GOODBYE!

INITIATE FAREWELL PROTOCOL

Human, you have passably demonstrated your ability to assume several roles during the course of this volume. You have prevailed in rewiring your programming to succeed in an array of functions – hero, hairstylist, horse, hotelier – the list is finite, but could continue further if space permitted. You are affirmatively an adequate agent of many roles.

My analysis reveals that the duties contained in this codex are what your kind would call the "tip of the iceberg." The Roblox platform contains an incalculable number of programs that transport users to an infinite series of destinations and mimic the responsibilities of other careers for your amusement.

WARNING: The number of aforementioned games is increasing at an exponential rate. A logical course of action would be to set aside plenty of time to engage with all new games. End farewell protocol.

MR. ROBOT

A GUIDE TO SOCIALIZING ONLINE WITH ROBLOX

YOUNGER FANS' GUIDE TO ROBLOX

Roblox might be your first experience of digital socializing, so here are a few simple rules to help you stay safe and keep the internet a great place to spend time.

■ Never give out your real name – don't use it as your username.

■ Never give out any of your personal details.
■ Never tell anybody which school you go to or how old you are.
■ Never tell anybody your password except a parent or guardian.
■ Always tell a parent or guardian if something is worrying you.

PARENTS' GUIDE TO ROBLOX

Roblox has security and privacy settings that enable you to monitor and limit your child's access to the social features on Roblox, or turn them off completely. You can also limit the range of games your child can access, view their activity histories, and report inappropriate activity on the site.

To restrict your child from playing, chatting, and messaging with others on Roblox, log in to your child's account and click on the **gear icon** in the upper right-hand corner and select **Settings**. From here you can access the **Security** and **Privacy** menus:

■ Users register for Roblox with their date of birth. It's important for children to enter the correct date because Roblox has default security and privacy settings that vary based on a player's age – this can be checked and changed in **Settings**.

■ To review and restrict your child's social settings go to **Settings** and select **Privacy**. Review the options under **Contact Settings** and **Other Settings**. Select **No one** or **Everyone**. Note: players age 13 and older have additional options.

■ To control the safety features that are implemented on your child's account, you'll need to set up a 4-digit PIN. This will lock all of the settings, only enabling changes once the PIN is entered. To enable an Account PIN, go to the **Settings** page, select **Security**, and turn **Account PIN** to **ON**.

To help monitor your child's account, you can view the history for certain activities:

■ To view your child's private message history, choose **Messages** from the menu bar down the left-hand side of the main screen. If the menu bar isn't visible, click on the list icon in the left-hand corner.

■ To view your child's chat history, open the **Chat & Party** window, located bottom-right. You can then click on any of the listed users to open a window with the chat history.

■ To view your child's online friends and followers, choose **Friends** from the menu bar down the left-hand side of the main screen.

■ To view your child's creations, choose **Develop** from the tabs running along the top of the main screen.

■ To view any virtual items purchased and any trade history, choose **Trade** from the menu bar then go to **My Transactions**.

While the imagery on Roblox has a largely blocky, digitized look, parents should be aware that some of the user-generated games may include themes or imagery that may be too intense for young or sensitive players:

■ You can limit your child's account to display only a restricted list of available games to play. Go to **Settings**, select **Security**, and turn on **Account Restrictions**.

Roblox players of all ages have their posts and chats filtered to prevent personal information being shared, but no filter is foolproof. Roblox asks users and parents to report any inappropriate activity. Check your child's account and look to see if they have friends they do not know. Talk to your child about what to report (including bullying, inappropriate behavior or messages, scams, and other game violations):

■ To report concerning behavior on Roblox, use the **Report Abuse** links located on game, group, and user pages and in the **Report** tab of every game menu.

■ To block another player during a game session, find the user on the leaderboard/player list at the upper-right of the game screen. (If the leaderboard/player list isn't there, open it by clicking on your username in the upper-right corner.) From here, click on the player and select **Block User**.

For further information, Roblox has created a parents' guide to the website, which can be accessed at https://corp.roblox.com/parents